BALLET

Kate Castle

KING*f*ISHER

NEW YORK

KINGFISHER
Larousse Kingfisher Chambers Inc.
80 Maiden Lane
New York, New York 10038
www.kingfisherpub.com

First published in hardcover in 1996
First published in paperback in 2001
10 9 8 7 6 5 4 3 (HC)
10 9 8 7 6 5 4 3 2 1 (PB)

1TR/1201/GC/PW(MA)/128CHST

LIBRARY OF CONGRESS CATALOGING-
IN-PUBLICATION DATA
Castle, Kate.
  Ballet / Kate Castle.—1st ed.
  p. cm.
  Includes index.
  Summary: An introduction to
  ballet, discussing its history,
  costumes, steps, performances,
  and other aspects.
  1. Ballet—Juvenile literature. [1. Ballet.]
  1. Title.
GV1787.5.C37 1996
792.8—dc20 96—5986 CIP AC

ISBN 0-7534-5001-1 (HC)
ISBN 0-7534-5488-2 (PB)

Consultant: Robert Greskovic
Editor: Camilla Hallinan
Design: Terry Woodley, Steve Leaning,
  Robert Perry
Art editor: Christina Fraser, Sue Aldworth
Picture research: Elaine Willis,
  Alex Goldberg

Printed in Hong Kong/China

CONTENTS

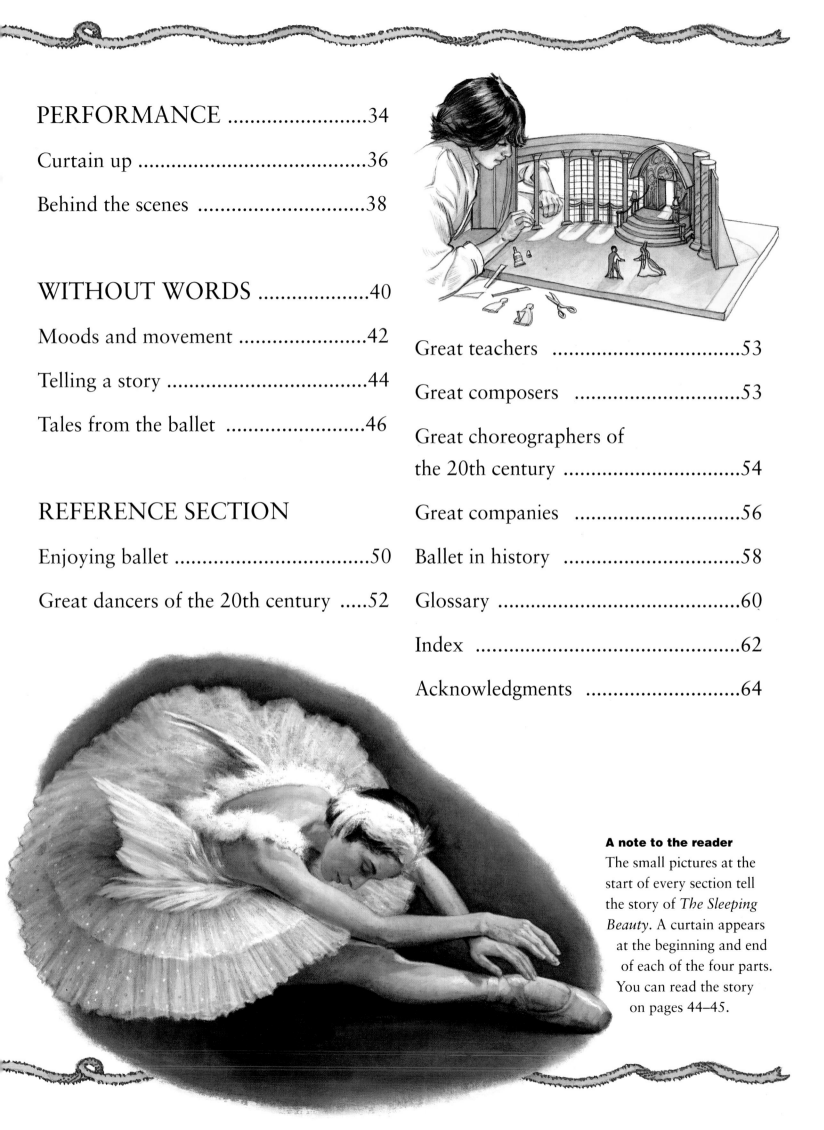

A note to the reader

The small pictures at the start of every section tell the story of *The Sleeping Beauty*. A curtain appears at the beginning and end of each of the four parts. You can read the story on pages 44–45.

THE STORY
OF DANCE

 All over the world people dance. Dance has always been at the center of important events such as marriage, the birth and naming of a child, and the burial of the dead. There are dances for sowing crops, gathering harvests, and making rain. Dance, songs, and the rhythmic sounds of drums and other instruments form rituals that draw people closer together.

NORTH AMERICA
1 Buffalo dance
2 Cheerleader
3 Square dance
4 Chinese New Year dragon dance
5 Tap dance

SOUTH AMERICA
6 Amazon tribal dance
7 Latin American ballroom dancing
8 Devil dance, Bolivia
9 Samba, Brazil

EUROPE
10 Morris dancers, U.K.
11 Flamenco, Spain
12 Scottish dancing
13 Irish dancing
14 Wedding dance, Turkey

AFRICA
15 Egyptian stick dance
16 Masked funeral dance, Dogon tribe
17 Tutsi dancers
18 Gambian dancers
19 Zulu war dance

ASIA
20 Mongolian "wrestlers" (dancer and puppet)
21 Khon dance drama, Thailand

4

All kinds of dance

Dance that belongs to a particular country is called folk dance. It is part of everyday life, celebrations, and ceremonies. Dance that is purely for pleasure and takes place at parties or clubs and in ballrooms is called social dance. Performance dance takes place on stage, film, or television for others to watch. It uses a mixture of dance, music, and design to tell a story or create a mood. There are many styles of performance dance —contemporary, jazz, tap, and ballet.

▶ Basilio and Kitri are the principal characters in *Don Quixote*, a ballet set in Spain. Kitri is en pointe, on the tips of her toes, but the ballet steps are performed in a style borrowed from Spain. The term "ballet" comes from the Italian word "ballo," meaning dance.

Ballet is different from other ways of dancing in two main respects: turn-out, in which the leg is turned at the hip so that the feet point sideways, and point work, in which ballerinas use specially stiffened shoes to stand on the very tips of their toes. Both turn-out and point work make certain movements, such as turns, easier to do and more spectacular to watch.

22 Kathak dance, India
23 Indian classical
24 Malay rice dance
25 Court dance, Java
26 Harvest dance, Japan
27 Bugaku, Japan
28 Kandy dancer, Sri Lanka
29 Temple dancer, Bali
OCEANIA
30 Aboriginal spear dance, Australia
31 All-Black haka, based on Maori war dance, New Zealand
32 Cook Islander
33 Hula dance, Hawaii

The beginning of ballet

Ballet began in the European courts of the 16th and 17th centuries. The court of Louis XIV of France was based at the splendid Palace of Versailles, just outside Paris. Courtiers took part in elaborate celebrations staged in gardens and ballrooms, called *ballets de cour*. These often had parades of horses, processions, speeches, and songs as well as dance.

▼ The courtly rules of behavior gave ballet much of its elegance and precision.

▼ Louis XIV danced in his first ballet when he was thirteen. His most famous role was as the sun god Apollo in *Le Ballet Royale de la Nuit* in 1653. The ballet lasted over 12 hours!

Greece and Rome

The ancient Greeks and Romans danced for pleasure, as illustrated in this frieze. Many of the early ballets were based on Greek and Roman legends.

A ballet called *The Loves of Mars and Venus* (the Roman gods of war and love) was performed in London in 1717. It was one of the first ballets to tell a story without using speech and song.

▲ **Frieze with a dancing bacchante, 425 B.C.**

Stars on the stage

Marie Camargo (1710–1770) shortened her skirt so that she could dance more difficult steps and show off her footwork.

Salvatore Vigano (1769–1821) and Maria Medina, his wife, wanted to bring more natural, expressive movements into ballet. They wore costumes based on those of ancient Greece.

When ballet began to be performed in theaters, at first as part of opera, professional dancers took the place of courtiers. In 1661, Louis XIV founded the Académie Royale de Danse. Its director, Pierre Beauchamp, recorded the steps and positions, including the five positions of the feet, which form the basis of today's technique.

Gaetano Vestris and his son Auguste were Italians who danced in France to huge acclaim in the 18th and 19th centuries. Gaetano was known as "the god of dance," but Auguste also astonished audiences with his virtuoso jumps and turns.

Ballet develops

By the 1830s, the costume for the ballerina looked as it does today in Romantic ballets like *La Sylphide*. The ballerina wore a long tutu with a fitted bodice and soft net skirts ending below the knee. Her hair was parted in the middle, draped over the ears, and drawn into a low bun. Early in the 20th century, as the steps became more daring, ballerinas began wearing the classical tutu, with short fluffy skirts of many layers which enhanced the steps.

En pointe
Marie Taglioni (1804–1884) was one of the first ballerinas to stand on the tips of her toes, *en pointe*, to look as if she were floating. Ballet shoes in those days were soft, so standing en pointe was very difficult. Her father, who was also her teacher, invented exercises to strengthen her legs and feet.

Romantic ballet
Romantic ballet was a reaction against all that was going on in the world. The introduction of factories and machines during the Industrial Revolution made choreographers want to write ballets that were light, airy, and unreal.

Romantic ballets were about fairies and spirits and humans rising above the world. Women were seen as delicate creatures who need protecting and lifting gently.

La Sylphide is one of the oldest Romantic ballets, and it is still danced today. It tells the story of a young Scot named James who falls in love with a Sylph. You can read their story on page 46.

Late in the 19th century, choreographer Marius Petipa devised a series of Classical ballets—grand and elaborate story ballets with lavish scenery and costumes. The stories are told through set patterns, a combination of solos for one person, *pas de deux* for two people, and small and large groups of dancers in the *corps de ballet*. Modern ballets don't always have a story. Instead they can be about moods and feelings.

Classical ballet

Ballerinas' steps are more daring and difficult in Classical ballet than in Romantic ballet.

In Act III of the Classical ballet *Swan Lake*, Odile tries to persuade Prince Siegfried that she is Odette, the Swan Queen he has fallen in love with. Odile wears a black tutu, whereas Odette wears white.

Rite of Spring

Vaslav Nijinsky created a ballet about a primitive human sacrifice which shocked audiences at its first performance in Paris in 1913. With its harsh theme, it became a turning point in both ballet and music. Since then, many choreographers have used Stravinsky's dramatic music to create their own *Rite of Spring*. The costumes in this production by Kenneth MacMillan allow the dancers total freedom of movement.

Modern ballet

The dancers create dramatic pictures in *Apollo*, a ballet by George Balanchine. Their costumes are more fitted, to show the shapes the dancers make. Apollo was a Greek god, and the three women represent mime, dance, and poetry. This type of ballet, modern but with classical steps, is sometimes called neo-classical.

The dancer

Dancers are special people. They are intelligent, musical, and adaptable. They have the confidence to dance solos but still work as part of a team. They use imagination to create different characters on stage. They take criticism without making a fuss, knowing that they will never stop learning and perfecting their technique. Lastly, all dancers enjoy challenges, pushing themselves and their technique to new limits by working with many different choreographers.

▶ **Mikhail Fokine created the _Dying Swan_ solo for Anna Pavlova for a charity performance in Russia. When she was dying of pneumonia in 1931, she is said to have whispered, "Prepare my Swan costume." The day after Anna Pavlova died, the cello music by Saint-Saens was played while the spotlight moved over the empty stage.**

A star is born

Anna Pavlova was born in St. Petersburg, Russia, in 1881. She was a frail, premature baby, and her mother was a poor widow. When she was eight, Anna's mother took her to see _The Sleeping Beauty_ at the Maryinsky Theater for a Christmas treat.

Anna knew immediately that she wanted to be a dancer and two years later joined the ballet school on Theater Street. With the help of teachers such as Enrico Cecchetti she worked hard, grew strong, and was accepted for the Maryinsky company.

Next stop the world

Pavlova had a special love for dancing that made her stand out from the rest. She wanted as many people as possible to enjoy her dancing—so for 15 years she danced all over the world, for rich people and poor, in large towns and small, traveling over 115,000 miles (185,000 km) and giving over 4,000 performances. She is remembered by all who saw her.

▶ Mikhail Baryshnikov, in Frederick Ashton's Rhapsody. Baryshnikov was born in 1948 and studied at the Kirov Ballet School. He moved to the West in 1976, and danced first with The Royal Ballet. One of the great virtuoso dancers of our century, he enjoyed working in film and with new choreographers. He directed the American Ballet Theatre in the 1980s, and now directs his own modern dance company, White Oak Dance Project.

◀ Another great ballerina, Margot Fonteyn, later described Pavlova as "a genius."

When dancers stop dancing, usually in their mid-thirties, they must take up a new career. Many become teachers, choreographers, or directors. Others stay close to the company by becoming physical therapists, administrators, or notators. The discipline of ballet prepares dancers well for a range of different careers.

"I desire that my message of beauty and joy and life shall be taken up and carried on after me. I hope that when Anna Pavlova is forgotten, the memory of her dancing will live with the people. If I have achieved even that little for my art, I am content." (Pavlova)

LEARNING TO DANCE

You can enjoy ballet classes without wanting to become a professional dancer. Ballet will give you confidence, poise, and an approach to learning that will be useful in all sorts of other areas. It is important to have the right attitude to your lessons—to look, listen, and keep trying even if it seems hard at first. Most important of all, lessons should be fun—something you and your teacher can both enjoy.

▼ This class started with exercises at the barre and has now moved into the center of the studio to continue without the barre.

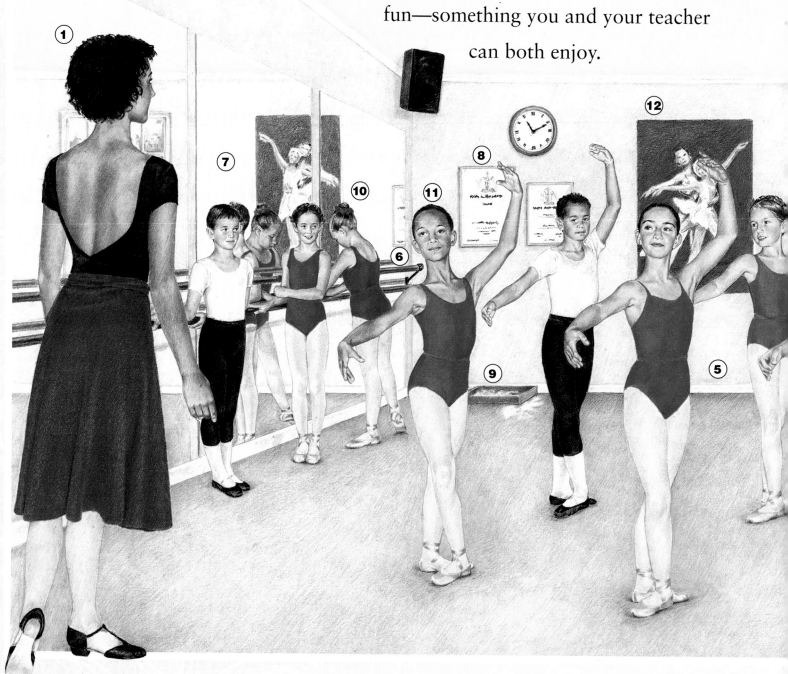

1 The teacher gives encouragement and corrections to the pupils.

2 The pianist plays music.

3 If the pianist is away, the teacher uses tapes.

4 The ends of your shoe ribbons must always be neatly tucked in.

5 The class is doing a *port de bras* exercise.

6 Pupils hold the barre to steady themselves during barre exercises.

7 Mirrors help the pupils to check their positions and alignments.

8 The teacher has certificates showing she has passed examinations and is qualified to teach.

9 A rosin box, filled with a powder that stops feet from slipping on the floor.

10 One pupil is practicing a different exercise while the others watch the class.

11 This pupil is holding her head in the correct position. Can you spot why the others are incorrect?

12 A colorful poster reminds the pupils what they are aiming for.

◄ The painter and sculptor Edgar Degas enjoyed watching dancers at the Paris Opéra Ballet in the late 19th century. This bronze figure is called *La Petite Danseuse* ("The Little Dancer"). She is 14 years old and is standing in fourth position. Is her posture correct? (Turn to page 17 to find out.)

When you begin to learn ballet you need to find a school with a qualified teacher. A qualification shows that they have taken exams in how to teach and have studied anatomy, so that they understand how the growing human body works. They may teach slightly different techniques, such as the Royal Academy of Dancing (RAD) or the Cecchetti method. Some schools offer the chance to take examinations, so you can check your progress. In addition to ballet, most schools offer classes in other styles such as modern, jazz, and tap.

▶ Class ends with a révérence, a bow that says "thank you" to the teacher and the pianist. This is preparation for acknowledging the applause of an audience.

What to wear

For your first lesson you can usually dance barefoot in something loose and comfortable. After that, most schools prefer you to wear a standard outfit, called practice clothes. Practice clothes fit as closely as possible so that the teacher can see the position of your body clearly and correct any mistakes. Everyone tries to be as neat and well groomed as possible.

Hair

The ballet hair style shows as much of the face as possible and makes the head look sleek and in proportion to the rest of the body. Long hair can be pinned into a bun or braided and pinned on top of the head. A short style can be kept neat with a headband. Dancing would be much harder with your hair tangling in your face.

▶ **Boys wear T-shirts or leotards, tights, and black or white leather ballet shoes with elastic, not ribbons.**

Getting ready

Use a bag to carry your practice clothes to class. Wash them each time they are worn and repair any shoe ribbons that may have come unstitched. Tuck shoes inside each other between classes to keep their shape.

Legwarmers and crossover sweaters are usually worn only at the beginning of class, tutus at performances, and jewelry never!

Shoe ribbons

Each ribbon is about 1 inch (2.5cm) wide and 20 inches (50cm) long. Fold the heel of the shoe forward. Sew a ribbon on each side, just in front of the fold. Sew to the canvas, not through the drawstring.

14

◀ Girls wear a leotard, tights, or socks (pink or white) and ballet shoes of canvas, leather, or satin. Nylon ribbons are sewn onto the shoes.

▶ It takes a skilled artisan ten minutes to make one pair of point shoes. Then they are baked hard for 14 hours at 140°F (60°C).

When you go en pointe depends on strength and aptitude, not age. The teacher will know when a student has the physical strength to lift her body weight off the tips of her toes by pulling up through the knees and out from the hips without straining. Going en pointe too early, or trying at home, can cause a painful injury.

Point shoes

In a ballet company each dancer will have her own supply of point shoes, stored for her either at the theater or in large baskets when on tour. She will use about ten pairs a month, although principal dancers may use twenty!

draw-string

linen lining

leather sole

satin covering

layers of burlap and glue

1 Keep your foot flat on the floor and start with the inside ribbon.

2 Loop the ribbon over the foot, around the ankle, and to the back again.

3 Cross the other ribbon over the first one, over the foot, around the ankle.

4 Tie a knot on the inside of your ankle and tuck in the ends neatly.

At the barre

All ballet classes begin at the barre, then move to the center for more difficult steps. The barre acts as a support while doing exercises that warm up the muscles and prepare for the steps which come later. Much of the time at the barre is spent working on turn-out and developing good placement, or placing. This is the relationship of one part of your body to another—for example, shoulders to hips. The teacher will correct any mistakes, and you can use the mirror to help check your positions.

Hands and feet

Hands are held with the fingers softly grouped together and the thumb tucked in. For an arabesque, the fingers can be flatter and more stretched (see page 18).

Feet point straight, as if through the middle toe. Toes mustn't be clenched. A foot that curves inward is called a sickle foot.

Eyes look straight ahead. Head is level, with the feeling of a long neck.

The arm is in second position. It slopes gently down from the shoulder, which must not be hunched up.

This is the working leg. The leg is stretched and the knee is straight.

The arm is in third position (RAD) or fifth en avant (Cecchetti method). The dancer is finishing a plié.

Knees bend and point to the side. If this hurts or is hard to do, then your feet are turned out too far.

Turn-out is from the hip, but the hips should stay flat to the front, not twisted or lifted so that one is higher than the other.

This is the supporting leg.

1 The first exercise is the *plié*. This is a *demi*, or half, plié in second position. Pliés improve turn-out and gently stretch the muscles.

Feet turn out, heels remain flat on the floor. They lift in a *grand*, or full, plié only in first, third, fourth, and fifth positions.

2 In *battements tendues*, the foot slides across the floor, stretching to a point. This strengthens the feet and legs, ready for neat and fast footwork later.

Posture

Pull your seat under and stomach up so your back is straight. Keep your head straight and your chin level. Feel that your neck is long and graceful and your shoulders are in a natural and comfortable position.

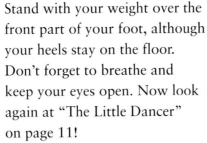

Stand with your weight over the front part of your foot, although your heels stay on the floor. Don't forget to breathe and keep your eyes open. Now look again at "The Little Dancer" on page 11!

Hard work and strain must not show in a dancer's face.

4 *Grands battements* strengthen the legs and improve turn-out and extension—the height the legs can be raised.

Knee points to the side, thigh well turned out.

Foot is flexed and gently rests on the ankle of the supporting leg before striking the floor.

Foot stays flat on the floor. If your ankle rolls inward, then your other leg has been lifted too high.

Leg is stretched, knee straight, foot pointed. Lift as high as it will go without raising your hip too much out of line.

3 In *battements frappés*, the ball of the foot strikes the floor sharply. In double battement frappé, the heel first crosses behind the ankle and back again. These help with more complicated footwork.

Exercises at the barre are practiced first on one leg and then on the other, turning around in between so that both sides of the body grow equally strong. Most exercises are done to the front, the side, the back, and the side again, known as *en croix*—in the shape of a cross.

Now look again at "The Little Dancer" on page 11!

Positions of the feet

Most ballet steps begin and end in one of the five positions of the feet. There are also five positions of the arms.

First position

Second position

Third position

Fourth position

Fifth position

When you first start, barre exercises take about 15 minutes, but professional dancers are strong enough to work at the barre for half an hour.

Center work

After the barre, some of the exercises are repeated without the support of the barre to improve strength, suppleness, and stamina. They begin with *ports de bras* for graceful arms, and *adage*, slow, sustained movements for poise and balance. This is followed by *pirouettes*, or turns, then *petit allegro* with *batterie*, quick small steps in which the legs are beaten together. Lastly comes *grand allegro*, traveling and jumping steps which feel like real dancing.

Pirouette en dehors from fifth position

Turns

A pirouette is a plié followed by a combined rise onto demi point and spin. Pirouettes can turn away from the supporting leg, *en dehors*, or toward, *en dedans*. You can also turn in other positions such as in arabesque.

In arabesque, a basic pose in ballet, one leg stretches up behind the dancer.

Dancers avoid becoming giddy by "spotting"— looking at a fixed spot at eye level for as long as possible, then whipping the head around quickly to find the spot again.

▼ First arabesque

The teacher

Ballet teachers have always been important. Some have developed the technique, others have helped famous dancers reach their full potential. Although your teacher may criticize you at times, he or she is there to help you dance your very best. Even world-famous principals who have a class every day make mistakes—but they never give up!

From 1906 to 1908, Anna Pavlova was Enrico Cecchetti's only pupil.

Adage

Draw an imaginary line with your finger from the dancer's extended hand to the tip of her toe, and another from the top of her head down to her supporting foot. Practicing adage helps to shape these positions.

Petit Allegro

This is a *changement*, which means "changing." Start in fifth position, jump, and change the feet once, landing in fifth position with the other foot in front. You can change the feet in the air up to three times, which is called an *entrechat six* (3x2 legs). Wayne Sleep has performed an amazing *entrechat douze* (6x2 legs).

Changement

When you are learning ballet, the exercises and steps may be much the same every week, especially if you are preparing for an exam. In a professional class, the teacher will set different *enchaînements*, or series of steps, to test the dancers' skill and memory. This also prepares them for working with a variety of choreographers.

Petit Allegro

Pas de chat means "step of the cat." One leg leads and the other follows as you jump sideways, swiftly and lightly like a cat. In the middle of this step, both legs are off the ground, pointed toes meeting in the air.

Pas de chat

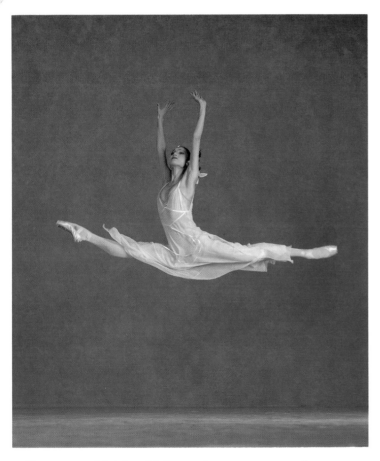

▲ **For a grand jeté, which means "big jump," both arms and legs are fully stretched. The dancer's body forms three curves:** two curves are from hands to feet, and one curve is from foot to foot. This leap is from the *The Fountain of Bakhchisarai.*

Grand Allegro

Temps de poisson means "fish's step" and looks as if a salmon is jumping out of the water in a silvery curve. Trace the shape the dancer makes with your finger and follow it with your eyes. The height of the jump is called its elevation.

▶ **A temps de poisson performed by Prince Siegfried in *Swan Lake*, Act III**

Pas de deux

 Pas de deux, or double work, is usually taught in a separate class. It consists of pirouettes, adage, and a huge variety of lifts performed with a partner. In Classical ballets, such as *The Sleeping Beauty*, pas de deux follow a set pattern: supported adage, male solo, and then female solo, usually ending with a faster finale called a coda. The man's role is to lift the woman and support her through a series of adage steps and turns. In later ballets, the choreography is more flowing and the lifts more acrobatic.

Supported arabesque

A ballerina can stand longer en pointe in arabesque with a partner's support. If the partner walks around her, while she keeps her balance, this is called a promenade.

▼ **Aurora and Prince Florimund, in a *Sleeping Beauty* pas de deux.**

Perfect partners

The audience appreciates the line of the pas de deux, both dancers making curves that balance or contrast with each other in intriguing shapes. Above all, pas de deux should look effortless.

Great partnerships

Two dancers may build a strong relationship, each improving the other's performance. Great partnerships include Margot Fonteyn and Rudolf Nureyev, Anthony Dowell and Antoinette Sibley, Peter Martins and Suzanne Farrell.

Finger fouettés

The male dancer lightly holds the ballerina's middle finger above her head while she turns. She begins to turn by pushing off from the palm of her other hand in his.

Practicing pas de deux means learning to trust your partner. Partners should be carefully matched in size. Coaching in pas de deux is usually given by former principal dancers, who make sure that the choreography is danced in the correct style. Pas de deux from the Romantic period are soft and flowing. Classical pas de deux are known for their elegance, clean line, and greater virtuosity.

Présage lift

The male dancer lifts the ballerina over his head with straight arms. She can do very little to help him, apart from jumping at the beginning of the lift, so this position needs great strength.

◄ Full of daring lifts, the Russian ballet *Spartacus* tells the story of a revolt led by a Roman slave.

Traveling lift

As the woman jumps, her partner lifts and carries her across the stage, in a graceful position which she sometimes changes in mid-air. As he supports her, she must keep the line of the jump.

▼ In *Voluntaries*, a modern ballet by Glen Tetley, experienced dancers can experiment with more daring and difficult lifts.

Getting stronger

Male dancers build strength in arms, shoulders, knees, and back by weight lifting and muscle-building exercises at ballet school, which must be properly taught to avoid injury. But boys should also remain streamlined for speed and agility. Too much bulk will spoil a dancer's line.

Sarah is eleven. She attended a special ballet school in England that teaches ordinary subjects too. She entered it after leaving elementary school. Before that she had been to weekly ballet classes with a local teacher. Competition to enter the school is fierce. Sarah had to audition by dancing in a class taught by a teacher from the school. Then doctors checked that her body was suitable for training. She will stay at the school until she is about sixteen, then move on to the senior school.

A day at ballet school

Sarah's day

This has been the very best day since I came to the ballet school. It took me a while to settle in when I first started six weeks ago. It was so strange to be living away from home and all my friends and family. But it's great to be with people who really understand how much I love dancing and don't get bored when I keep talking about it!

The day began, as usual, with an enormous breakfast at eight o'clock—no dieting here—we need to eat lots of healthful food to help our bones grow strong. We had our daily class from nine to ten-thirty and Ms. Farmer said that my pas de chats were very messy—my fifth positions looked more like thirds. But I did a perfect double pirouette, so that made me feel better. My friends stayed behind after class and we helped each other to practice. The girls have daily ballet class together, but the boys will

first, a big breakfast!

Ms. Farmer's class

join us tomorrow for an hour of character dancing. We are learning some of the mazurka steps from Act I of *Coppélia*. We have school lessons as well, just like any other school, and I like math, music, and French. It really helps to know that "pas de chat" means cat's step, for example, and that "glisser" means to slide.

After lunch we had more schoolwork, and later in the afternoon, at four, we had an hour's point-work class, where we are learning how to rise onto point holding on to the barre. While we did this, the boys practiced lifting weights to help them build their muscles for pas de deux. My partner is named William. He's thirteen, the same age as my brother, and he likes the same sorts of things—rock bands, football, computer games.

Supper was at six; and then, when we'd all done our homework and sewn the ribbons on our new shoes, the principal told us that the company has chosen some students to be in the new production of *The Nutcracker*. The school is linked to the company, so we are sometimes allowed to watch rehearsals or take part in the productions. I am to be a mouse in Act I! Even better, I am also to be the understudy for Clara, who has a solo and dances with the Nutcracker Prince. The first night is at the beginning of December, so we only have six weeks in which to practice. I can't wait until tomorrow when a teacher from the company comes to teach us the steps! The last two weeks of November we'll spend some time with the company, rehearsing first in the studio and then on stage. Scary!

character dancing

sewing ribbons

Natalie is sixteen. She will be in the senior school for two or three years, at the end of which she might be chosen for the company. The company staff will have watched Natalie closely throughout her training. Of the twenty-five girls in her class, probably only five will be picked for the company attached to the school. The rest will audition for other companies in Europe and abroad.

Natalie's Day

I sometimes wish I were still at the lower school, instead of living in this apartment where no one but me ever seems to do the dishes. Life at the upper school is very hard work. The day's schedule is crammed full, and then we have to shop, cook, and wash our own clothes—a bit like being in the company and away on tour.

I'm late!

Anya and I were late for nine o'clock class this morning because we forgot to set the alarm. The teacher was a guest from the company, and he wasn't very pleased with us. Then we had pas de deux for an hour and began learning how to do fish dives. This was quite funny, as several of us ended up on the floor. Jamie, my partner, kept making me laugh, but we did it really well in the end.

After lunch we had a makeup class and then at the end of the day we had repertoire for another hour. The girls are learning corps de ballet work—the Snowflakes Waltz from *The Nutcracker*—while the boys are learning Colas's solo from *La Fille Mal Gardée*—the one with all the difficult turns. When we know *The Nutcracker* really well, we shall be able to watch the company rehearsals. Then, if someone is ill or injured we might go on stage in their place. Everyone hopes they will get into the company, but so few actually do.

our first fish dive

makeup

Although I like the older ballets, I enjoy the newer ones too. We had workshops at the lower school on how to create ballets, and I decided then that I would like to be a choreographer. I am making a new piece for a studio performance, and Jamie, Laura, and I worked on it all evening. I can see all the steps in my imagination, and it's so frustrating when they can't get it right. They keep asking what it's about, but it doesn't have a story as such. I've just called it "Two's Company." The music helps a lot. A music student has written it specially, and it's very loud with electronic synthesizers and strange effects.

After the rehearsal, Laura and I walked home. Since it was after nine, we picked up a huge pizza on the way. Must remember to set the alarm!

early to bed, early to rise

rehearsing

Teamwork

While the dancers practice in the rehearsal studio, hundreds of other people are busy in costume and scenery workshops, in the orchestra pit, and in the theater offices. It is this complex teamwork that finally brings a ballet to the stage.

1 The Director runs the company. He is watching a final studio rehearsal of a new production of *Swan Lake*.

2 The choreographer has made some alterations to the original choreography. He checks to see if the group position is correct.

3 The notator records the choreography using symbols, as in music notation.

4 The accompanist plays the piano version of the full orchestral score.

5 The conductor watches some of the final rehearsals so he knows the tempo—how fast or slow the music must be played.

6 The ballet mistress, a former dancer, is in charge of the corps de ballet and helps the dancers keep in line.

7 The ballet master runs some rehearsals and produces a schedule of rehearsals.

8 The understudies watch and learn. There are several sets of dancers, or casts, for each ballet, and they each take turns in performing.

9 A soloist practices an attitude at the barre. She is cast as one of the Big Swans in Act II.

10 The sorcerer Von Rothbart, *Swan Lake*'s villain, waits to make his entrance.

11 A dancer fixes her shoe. As a coryphée, or junior soloist, she performs the Dance of the Little Swans with three others.

12 The corps de ballet must all keep in line in exactly the same position.

13 The répétiteur is a former principal dancer who now coaches principals.

14 The principal female dancer, a prima ballerina, dances in the two roles of Odette and Odile.

15 The principal male dancer, a premier danseur, is Prince Siegfried. He is a guest artist from another company.

CREATING A BALLET

Ballet is a combination of dancing, music, costumes, scenery, and lighting. A new ballet is the result of a close partnership among many people. First there is the choreographer, who has the idea for the ballet and devises the steps. He works closely with the composer, who writes the music or decides what sounds to use. Then there are the designers of scenery, costumes, and lighting, who decide how the ballet will look on stage. Even classics, such as *Swan Lake*, can have new scenery and costumes.

▲ Edgar Degas' "The Dancing Class" shows that ballerinas used to rehearse in tutus, not in the kind of practice clothes they wear now.

The composer and choreographer

Many things give choreographers ideas for ballets—myths, legends, poetry, plays, even the Bible. These ideas are expressed in movement shaped by music. Sometimes the choreographer commissions new music from a composer. He outlines his ideas, and the composer responds with music that the choreographer can work with. Modern ballet music may use electroacoustic instruments and unusual sounds to create its effect.

Pyotr Ilyich Tchaikovsky (1840–1893)

A composer

Tchaikovsky wrote lyrical and dramatic music for the Imperial Russian Ballet, including such masterpieces as *Swan Lake*, *The Sleeping Beauty*, and *The Nutcracker*. Choreographer Petipa would give Tchaikovsky detailed notes, counting out the numbers of bars of music he needed for each mime or series of steps.

A choreographer

Marius Petipa studied first with his father and then with Auguste Vestris at the Paris Opéra. He became Ballet Master in St. Petersburg in 1869. His ballets include *Swan Lake*, *The Sleeping Beauty*, and *The Nutcracker*. They are known for their spectacular divertissements, with demanding virtuoso steps, and for their complex corps de ballet scenes.

Marius Petipa (1818–1910)

Orchestral score and dance notation for *Swan Lake*

Sometimes a choreographer will have heard existing music, which she feels is just right for ballet. By listening to it frequently, she begins to see stage pictures taking shape in her imagination. The company notator works alongside the choreographer, writing down the steps.

Serge Diaghilev brought composers and choreographers together to create new ballets which delighted and shocked audiences. His company, the Ballets Russes de Serge Diaghilev, performed from 1909 to 1929 and changed ballet from old-fashioned romance and fairy tales to modern emotions and vivid color.

▲ **This is the Benesh notation for a grand jeté from *La Bayadère*,**

Notation is a way of writing down the steps of a ballet. Labanotation is widely used in the United States and can record any movement, not just dance.

Petipa's ballet about a young Indian warrior's love for a temple dancer.

This is an example of the other system, Benesh notation. Dancers also use video to help them learn and remember the steps.

▼ **Diaghilev watches a rehearsal of *Le Tricorne* ("The Three Cornered Hat"),** **a ballet set in Spain about a miller and his wife.**

Choreographer Léonide Massine works with Tamara Karsavina, one of the greatest ballerinas of the Ballets Russes, and Leon Woizikowsky, a virtuoso dancer. Composer Manuel de **Falla is at the piano, and the artist Pablo Picasso has brought his designs. They all loved the beauty and mystery of Spain: Massine learned flamenco dancing to enrich his choreography.**

The Designer

Besides being able to use color, texture, and perspective in an imaginative way, a designer also has to be an architect and an engineer. Some sets have balconies, windows, and staircases, while others use machinery to move scenery. Sets must also be easy for the stage crew to change between acts and, in a touring production, load into vans. Most importantly, the stage and lighting design must help the audience to enter another world as it watches the ballet.

▲ A Paris Opéra design for Act II, *Swan Lake*, by Bouchère

1 The designer
The designer talks to the choreographer as soon as a new ballet is planned. He or she then draws detailed pictures of each scene of the ballet.

2 The model
The drawings are used to make scale models of each scene, complete with miniature furniture.

▼ Model for Act III, *Swan Lake*

◄ Backdrop for Acts II and IV, *Swan Lake*

3 The backdrop
Backdrops are painted either flat on the floor or hung vertically in a work-shop. A grid is laid over the design, which is then drawn section by section on the large, unpainted cloth.

The lighting designer brings even more atmosphere to the production, using colored lights, spotlights, and special effects. His lighting designs will be entered as a computer program operated at each performance by a technician seated in a control room at the back of the theater's auditorium.

4 The scenery

The designer keeps a close eye on the workshops as the set is being built. Skilled carpenters make the scenery, including the flats that stand at the side of the stage. They begin work many weeks ahead of the first performance.

5 The lights

The lights themselves are called a rig, and have to be set up before each performance. They are fixed on supports, called booms, at the side or hung from a bar above the stage. At a technical rehearsal, the lighting effects for each scene are created once the scenery is in place. The designer directs the rehearsal from a lighting desk in the auditorium.

A technician changes a gel, a colored but transparent slide that alters the color of a white lamp. The lamp's shutters are adjusted to alter the amount of light.

Props

Props is short for properties, objects the dancers will use in their hands on stage. They are made in the company's workshops. Props can be made of wood, cloth, papier-mâché, or acrylic resin. They are often much lighter than they look, yet need to be very hard-wearing, since each ballet can last for many years.

La Fille Mal Gardée: Alain's umbrella and bouquet

Cinderella: broomstick

Swan Lake: goblet

Romeo and Juliet: sword

The Nutcracker: nutcracker doll

The Sleeping Beauty: spindle

Costume and makeup

The costume designer is responsible for clothes, hats, shoes, wigs, jewelry, and often makeup too. A full-length ballet may need up to 300 costumes. The designer draws and colors a separate sketch for each one and writes suggestions for materials and trimmings such as lace, sequins, or beads on the design. Sometimes samples of fabric are stapled to the design before it goes to the workshops.

Which fabric?

Fabric looks different under stage lighting than in daylight, and the people who make the costumes know what materials give the best effect. Dyeing gives fabric exactly the right color, and new costumes can be "broken down" with paint to make them look worn, as with Cinderella's rags.

Cutting

A tutu may take a day and a half to assemble. First patterns are chalked onto fabric and cut out by skilled dressmakers.

Sewing

The costume is basted together with hand stitches, then sewn on a machine. Fastenings and trimmings are usually sewn on by hand.

Fitting

Each costume can last for many years and will probably be worn by many dancers. The costume is fitted on the dancer and any alterations are made. A label with the dancer's name on is then sewn into the costume.

▲ Nijinsky's costume in *Petrushka*, designed by Alexandre Benois for Diaghilev's Ballets Russes

◄ Odile's tutu, *Swan Lake*

Repairs

When Nijinsky danced in Fokine's *Le Spectre de la Rose* in 1911, his costume was sewn with petals in dusky pinks and browns to suggest the spirit of the rose. The costume constantly needed repairs because admirers of this great dancer took the petals as souvenirs.

▶ Dancing chickens in Frederick Ashton's ballet *La Fille Mal Gardée*

▼ Costume for Jeremy Fisher in Frederick Ashton's *Tales of Beatrix Potter*

◀ Ian Spurling designed colorful and witty costumes for Kenneth MacMillan's ballet *Elite Syncopations*, which is set to ragtime music by Scott Joplin.

H owever elaborate the designs are, the dancers must still be able to move freely, lift their arms, turn, and jump in the costumes. A costume must also complement the dancer's shape—tutus that are too long and droopy can make the dancer's legs look short and spoil the choreography. A design can suggest a character without the costume being realistic.

Makeup

Odette
Under strong stage lighting, dancers' features disappear unless they are heavily made up.

Siegfried
Men wear makeup too.

Von Rothbart
The wicked magician creates a fantastic effect using many colors of makeup.

A dancer's diary

I still can't believe how quickly things have happened. One day it seemed as if I was going to be in the corps de ballet forever; the next day I had been cast for a leading role in a new full-length ballet. The choreographer was looking for someone new and liked my dancing. Since then, in some ways everything has changed, in others it's still the same and always will be.

"like this"

Business as usual

For example, every morning at ten-thirty I have class for ninety minutes, and the teacher still corrects my mistakes. No chance of getting big-headed! At the moment I'm working on my traveling turns, which can get a bit wobbly as I cross the stage *en diagonale*. After class I rehearse all day because I have lots of new ballerina roles to learn: Juliet and Cinderella this year, Aurora and Giselle next year. Sometimes these are solo or pas de deux rehearsals; other times it's a full call with all the company, either in the studio or on stage. I'm very fortunate because the répétiteurs who coach me in these roles are usually famous dancers themselves, who pass on their knowledge to me. There are regular costume fittings now, and each week I collect my new point shoes and prepare them. I use so many these days—at least three pairs a week—that I seem to be constantly sewing on ribbons.

I have to remember to fit meals in somewhere, usually salad and fruit for lunch, something to give me energy just before the show, and something a bit more substantial afterward. I might go out with my friends for pizza and my favorite dessert. Now that I'm a principal, I usually perform on stage only once or twice a week. On the other nights I might go to a Broadway show or a movie— I learn so much from watching others perform.

a new role

Fame

When I was dancing the Sugar Plum Fairy in *The Nutcracker* last Christmas, I was interviewed for children's television and answered a phone-in about ballet. Then, when I first became a principal dancer, several newspapers wanted to interview me. Journalists always ask if I'm nervous before a performance. Of course! Everyone is, but as soon as you see the audience and start dancing it just disappears. Now the whole world suddenly seems to be interested in me! I've modeled clothes for a Paris fashion designer and have just been photographed for a new book about ballet.

with the physical therapist

Injury

It's not all fun, though. Last year I had a stress fracture which took a long time to heal. I hated being injured, but at least it gave me time to catch up on replying to letters from people who have enjoyed my dancing. Thanks to the company physical therapist, I'm now fully recovered.

Going on tour

I'm glad I didn't miss the company's tour of Japan and Korea. We did a triple bill, a program of three short ballets: *Les Sylphides*, *Les Patineurs*, and *Stars and Stripes*. When we arrive in a different theater, there isn't usually time for a full stage rehearsal. Instead, the corps de ballet just walks through all its movements and groupings to see how it will fit onto the new stage. The principals also walk through their steps on stage and without music, which is called "marking." On tour we often have a first-night celebration—it's good to meet members of the audience and talk to them about the performance. Then it's back to the hotel to wash our practice clothes ready for class in the morning.

Dancing for the Queen

I have been asked to appear as a guest artist with one of the best ballet companies in Britain. The ballet they want me to dance, *Serenade*, is in our repertoire, but I'll still need to rehearse it with them

and adapt to their production. One of the performances will be a gala attended by the Queen. I'm sure the company will make me feel very welcome. Then it's back to New York and straight into class again, where I'll be working on those pirouettes. Back to earth with a bump!

Stars and Stripes

curtain call

A ballerina's year

January: Performances of *The Nutcracker*—Sugar Plum Fairy solo filmed for a television program.

February: Rehearsals and costume fittings for new ballet.

March: First performance of new ballet. Radio and television interviews.

April: Tour of Far East (Japan and Korea). Rehearsals for *Swan Lake*.

May: Return to N.Y.C. Performances of *Swan Lake*. Rehearsals for *Romeo and Juliet*.

July: *Romeo and Juliet* televised. Interviews for newspapers and magazines.

August: Vacation. No class or rehearsals.

September: Classes, rehearsals, and coaching for *Serenade*.

October: Guest artist in London performance of *Serenade*.

November: Rehearsals for *Cinderella*. New partner joins the company from Paris Opéra Ballet.

December: Performances of *Cinderella*. Meet audience after children's matinee.

PERFORMANCE

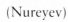 Golden lights glow in the auditorium. The heavy stage curtains are closed. People are talking quietly and reading their programs. There are ripples of music as musicians tune up in the orchestra pit. The lights grow dim and silence falls. The conductor enters and steps onto the podium. He lifts his baton—the audience seems to hold its breath. Then the orchestra begins to play the overture, lively music that sets the scene. Suddenly the curtain sweeps up and the stage is full of movement, color, and light.

Rudolf Nureyev saw his first ballet when he was seven. His family was very poor, and his mother could afford only one ticket. She took Rudolf and his three sisters along to the theater in the cold Russian winter, and in the last-minute rush before the doors were closed, she managed to squeeze the whole family into the theater. The experience was to change his life.

"I shall never forget a single detail of the scene which met my eyes; the theater itself with its soft, beautiful lights and gleaming crystal chandeliers; small lanterns hanging everywhere; colored windows; everywhere velvet, gold— another world; a place which, to my dazzled eyes, you could only hope to encounter in the most enchanted fairy tale. I was speechless. From that day I can truthfully date my unwavering decision to become a ballet dancer."

(Nureyev)

Swan Lake Act III

The evil Von Rothbart and his daughter, Odile, arrive at the ball, intent on deceiving Prince Siegfried. Odile has disguised herself as Odette, the beautiful Swan Queen whom Siegfried has promised to marry.

The stage manager runs the show. She calls dancers from their dressing rooms and works closely with the stage crew and front-of-house staff (ushers, box office, etc.) to make sure that everything runs smoothly.

The lighting desk is usually at the back of the auditorium. Technicians are in contact with backstage crew via a sound system and TV monitors.

Curtain up

The performance has begun. While the audience watches the ballet and listens to the music, behind the scenes everyone is hard at work, making the performance look as effortless as possible.

In the pit

The conductor uses the baton to show the orchestra how fast to play and to help them play together. He must also closely watch the dancers on stage and be aware of their needs.

During the intermission, the audience can relax, talk about the ballet, and read their programs. Backstage in their dressing rooms, the dancers hastily change costumes, shoes, and hairstyles. On stage, while the curtains are closed, the stage crew quickly and quietly changes the scenery for the next act.

The costume assistant is in the dressing room of the principal ballerina, checking her costume for the next act, when she will appear as Odette.

In the wings, a dancer from the Neapolitan duet gets her breath back. The other dancer checks her shoes before going on as the vision of Odette in the window of the ballroom.

The stage technicians are responsible for sound, lighting, scenery, props, and special effects. A large theater may need a team of more than 100 people.

Behind the scenes

Staging a ballet involves long-term planning, as far as five years ahead of the first performance. So while *Swan Lake* is under way, preparations have already begun for the next production. In a large theater like the Met, work never stops.

1 Billboards advertise *Swan Lake* and other performances. The marketing and press departments design programs, posters, and leaflets to promote performances.
2 The foyer or entrance lobby where the audience gathers.
3 Bars and a restaurant sell refreshments.
4 The auditorium seats 3,800 on four tiers and an orchestra level.
5 Ballet rehearsal room.
6 Offices—administration, press, and marketing.
7 The orchestra pit holds up to 110 musicians and can be raised to stage level for concerts.
8 The corps de ballet.
9 The principal dancers, Siegfried and Odette.
10 A spotlight operated by a lighting technician follows the principal dancers with a small pool of light. It isn't visible here, but the lighting and sound control booth is at the back of the auditorium on the orchestra level.

The Met

There has been a Metropolitan Opera House in New York since 1883. The new house at Lincoln Center opened in 1966. It presents both opera and ballet.

To give you an idea of the Met's size, the proscenium arch that frames the stage is the tallest in the world—54ft. high. To run a theater this big takes a big team—the Met employs about 1,000 people.

The stage manager's desk is to one side of the stage. It has TV monitors showing the stage and the conductor. A sound system calls dancers to the stage, cues the front-of-house staff, and communicates with the technicians.

11 The stage curtain.
12 The proscenium.
13 Lights are hung from four steel bridges above the stage. These bridges are big enough to hold the technicians who change the lights.
14 The backdrop, also known as the backcloth, is hung from the flies.

15 The backdrop for Act III waits to be lowered in the scene change during the intermission.
16 On either side of the stage, there are five fly galleries for lighting and clearing scenery.
17 The fly system uses over 100 battens of steel tubing for hanging the

backdrops and scenery, and is electronically controlled. Older theaters use weights and pulleys and more manpower.
18 The main stage is 100ft. (30m) wide and 83ft. (25m) deep. It has seven hydraulically operated platforms which can be raised and lowered separately.

19 The rear slip stage, with a revolving platform 59ft. (18m) in diameter.
20 The right slip stage, where scenery for the next act or for another production can be set up and slid into place. (The left slip stage is on the other side of the stage.)
21 Scenery from Act I.
22 The loading dock can take four trucks at a time, to load or unload scenery.
23 Opera rehearsal room.
24 In the chorus dressing room, each person has a place to make up at, with a mirror.

25 The carpentry workshop makes scenery and props. The scenery is painted in another area known as the paint shop, and is then taken by elevator down to an underground

storage area.
26 The electrical workshop does the heavy-duty metalwork for scenery and props, and maintains lighting, sound, and electronic equipment.
27 A wardrobe holding area stores and maintains costumes being used in

current productions.
28 The wig room is part of the costume shop, where new costumes are made, trimmed, and fitted.
29 The principals each have a dressing room with a shower, a sofa, a piano, and an audio paging system linked to the stage manager's desk.

Step by step

Watch for the patterns the steps make. They may be repeated, or one dancer will dance a step while the other seems to reply, like a conversation. Sometimes a group of dancers performs one series of steps together, while the soloist dances another in contrast or counterpoint. The same step can be danced in many different ways. All the different steps make up a kind of dance alphabet, which is the choreographer's vocabulary.

WITHOUT WORDS

 People going to their first ballet may worry whether they'll understand it. But as soon as the curtain goes up, they are swept along in the excitement. Most of the older ballets, such as *Swan Lake*, are narrative ballets—they tell stories. Acting, mime, and large group scenes help to move the action along. Some ballets have no story but instead follow a clear theme or idea.

▶ **Les Sylphides is a ballet in the Romantic style, but it was choreographed by Michel Fokine and first performed in 1909. It is a ballet with a theme but no story, and is set in moonlight near a ruined chapel.**

Abstract ballets have neither story nor theme. They use dance to create mood and atmosphere. In all ballets, look for color, pattern, shape, and imaginative use of steps. Notice how the music, scenery, and costumes are used together and you can find your own meaning.

▲ **Danses Concertantes is a lively modern ballet choreographed by Kenneth Macmillan to music by Stravinsky. It has no story or theme,** **but the unusual movements follow the music to make a ballet full of wit and fun.**

Moods and movement

To help yourself enjoy ballet more, ask yourself some questions as you watch. Are the dancers moving with strong, leaping steps across the stage on their own, or with small neat steps within a large group? Do they use sudden, darting steps or long, slow stretching movements? What do these movements and groupings seem to say?

Fun

Frederick Ashton's ballet *The Dream* is based on Shakespeare's play *A Midsummer Night's Dream*.

The naughty sprite Puck uses quick, light, traveling steps. Here, he turns his palms upward mischievously with his toe just touching the ground.

Joy

In Kenneth MacMillan's version of Shakespeare's play, Romeo and Juliet dance a joyful pas de deux in the garden beneath Juliet's balcony. She shows her trust in Romeo by letting him support her in this difficult lift.

You can also use the clues given by the music, costumes, scenery, and lighting. Is the stage a dark and mysterious blue, or is it bright and sunny? What do the dancers' costumes tell you about their character or mood? Does the music emphasize the movement or provide an unusual contrast? What are you feeling as you watch?

Fear

Crossed positions with limbs turned inward often show fear or sadness, while open positions show happiness or trust. Here, Prince Ivan captures the Firebird in Fokine's ballet. He holds her tightly as if to stop her wings from fluttering as she tries to escape. She looks fearfully back at him over her shoulder.

Sorrow

Petrushka, the unloved and unhappy puppet, kneels in misery with shoulders hunched and hands crossed. His head is tilted and his eyes look helplessly upward.

Mime from Giselle

Gesture and expression help to tell the story:
1 Giselle, Act I: "I can **hear** Albrecht coming to meet me."
2 Albrecht, Act I: "I **promise** to **love** you forever, Giselle."
3 Princess Bathilde, Act I: "I am engaged to **marry** Albrecht."
4 Myrthe, the Queen of the Wilis, Act II: "You shall **die**, Albrecht !"
5 Albrecht, Act II: "**Why** must I die? Have pity!"

Telling a story

*T*he Sleeping Beauty is a narrative ballet choreographed by Petipa in 1890 with music by Tchaikovsky. Petipa based the ballet on Charles Perrault's 17th-century fairy tale and told it in four sections—a prologue and three acts.

In Act I, Princess Aurora pricks her finger on the spindle and collapses. She is surrounded by the King and Queen, courtiers, and suitors. This is a *scène d'action*.

Thanks to the Lilac Fairy, Aurora is not dead, only in a deep sleep.

Danced by a soloist, the Lilac Fairy leads the fairies bringing gifts to the royal christening in the prologue. The King and Queen are character parts.

They use mime, not dance, to create their characters and tell the story. Usually the role of the bad fairy, Carabosse, is also played by a character dancer.

The roles of Aurora and Florimund are played by principal dancers, a prima ballerina and a premier danseur. Florimund finds the castle in Act II and wakes Aurora with a kiss.

In Act III, they dance a grand wedding pas de deux, followed by two solos and an exciting finale.

Angry at being left out of the christening, Carabosse uses mime to cast a spell: Aurora will prick her finger on a spindle and die. In some productions, this part is taken by a man.

Puss-in-Boots and the White Cat are usually danced by coryphées or junior soloists. These are called demi-caractère parts. They dance one of the divertissements during the wedding in Act III.

The Sleeping Beauty follows a pattern common to Petipa's narrative ballets. There are the scènes d'action, which tell the story clearly in acting and mime. Then the *pas d'action*, which use dance steps to show what the characters are feeling. As the story unfolds, it is interrupted by *divertissements*: displays of dancing for its own sake which are not really part of the story. Finally there are variations, which highlight a dancer's virtuoso skills.

Tales from the Ballet

La Sylphide
This version: 1836,
Copenhagen.
choreography: August
Bournonville
music: Herman von
Løvenskjold

James is a young Scottish farmer.
On the eve of his wedding to Effie,
a beautiful Sylphide (a forest fairy)
appears at his window. James is
now torn between his love for the
Sylphide and for Effie. The wedding
is celebrated with Highland dancing.
Before rings are exchanged, the
Sylphide lures James away. Effie
is in despair.

  A witch called Madge gives
James a magic scarf, to capture the
Sylphide. In the forest, James and
the Sylphide dance with the scarf.
James wraps it around her and
pulls her to him. The angry witch
has poisoned the scarf, and the
Sylphide's wings fall from her
body. Without them, she
will die.

Giselle
1841, Paris
choreography: Jean Coralli
and Jules Perrot
music: Adolphe Adam

Giselle loves "Loys," who is Count
Albrecht in disguise. The forester
Hilarion is bitterly jealous. As
Giselle dances, her mother warns she
might overtire herself and die, just
like the Wilis—the ghosts of girls
who died before their wedding day.
The duke and his daughter, Bathilde,
arrive. Giselle dances for them, and
discovers that "Loys" is engaged to
Bathilde. She dances wildly, then
dies at her mother's feet.

  The Wilis rise from their graves,
led by Myrtha, their Queen, and
dance in the moonlight. Hilarion
comes to Giselle's grave, and the
Wilis make him dance to his death.
Albrecht is also commanded to
dance, but Giselle, now a Wili
herself, dances for him. At dawn she
returns to her grave, and Albrecht
is spared.

Don Quixote
1869, Moscow
choreography: Marius
Petipa
music: Ludwig Minkus

There are several versions of this
ballet, based on a Spanish novel by
Cervantes. Don Quixote is an old
man bewitched by tales of knights in
shining armor who searches for
similar adventures of his own.

  In the Petipa ballet, the main
characters are the young lovers
Basilio and Kitri, who live in
Barcelona. Kitri is being forced by
her father to marry the rich
Gamache. Don Quixote arrives at
her father's inn, sees that Kitri is
unhappy, and challenges Gamache
to a duel—but the would-be knight
is chased away. Basilio pretends he is
dying, and begs Kitri's father to take
pity and grant him permission to
marry her—his wish is granted.

  During the wedding celebrations,
Basilio and Kitri perform a grand
pas de deux, in Spanish style, and
the ever-hopeful Don Quixote
departs for further
adventures.

Coppélia

1870, Paris
choreography:
Arthur Saint-Léon
music: Léo Delibes

Franz and Swanhilda live in a small town where Dr. Coppélius has a toyshop. His favorite doll, Coppélia, is so lifelike that Franz falls in love with her. Furious, Swanhilda creeps into the shop with her friends to investigate.

Suddenly Dr. Coppélius returns, so Swanhilda hides and changes into the doll's clothes. Franz climbs up a ladder to look at Coppélia. Dr. Coppélius grabs him, and with magic spells tries to use Franz's energy to make the doll come alive. Swanhilda pretends she is Coppélia and performs a Scottish and a Spanish dance. Then she sets all the clockwork toys to work to release Franz from a spell. They escape, leaving Dr. Coppélius heartbroken.

As the town celebrates a new bell with Dances of the Hours, Dawn, and Prayer, Swanhilda apologizes to Dr. Coppélius for her deception and dances with Franz.

The Sleeping Beauty

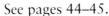

1890, St. Petersburg
choreography: Petipa
music: Pytor Ilyich
Tchaikovsky

See pages 44–45.

The Nutcracker

1892, Moscow
choreography: Lev Ivanov
music: Tchaikovsky

It is Christmas in Germany. A mysterious guest arrives at the Stahlbaums' party. It is Herr Drosselmeyer, with a soldier's uniform for Fritz, and a nutcracker in the shape of a soldier for Clara.

After the party, Clara creeps downstairs to fetch her nutcracker. Drosselmeyer appears, the clock stops, and the Christmas Tree and the toys grow huge and come alive. The Nutcracker does battle with the evil Mouse King, and Drosselmeyer changes him into a prince, who takes Clara on a magical journey.

First, they travel to the Land of Snow, where they meet the Snow Queen. Then they visit the Land of Sweets, where the Sugar Plum Fairy presents a series of divertissements for Clara: a coffee dance, a tea dance, Madame Bonbonnière, a Russian dance, and lastly the Waltz of the Flowers. The Prince and the Sugar Plum Fairy dance solos and a grand pas de deux before Clara suddenly finds herself back at home, wondering if it was all a dream.

Swan Lake

1877, Moscow
choreography: Acts
I and III by Petipa,
II and IV by Ivanov
music: Tchaikovsky

It is Prince Siegfried's 21st birthday. His mother tells him he must soon be married. He sets off for the forest.

By a lake deep in the forest, Siegfried sees a swan and takes aim to shoot, but the swan becomes a beautiful girl. She begs Siegfried not to shoot—she is Princess Odette and she and her companions have been turned into swans by Von Rothbart, an evil magician disguised as an owl. Only true love will save her. The Prince promises to love and marry her. ➡

Siegfried vows never to break his promise. They and the other swan-maidens dance until Von Rothbart draws them back to the lake and under his spell.

The Queen arranges a ball, and several princesses dance, but the Prince rejects them all. Suddenly a mysterious guest arrives. It is Von Rothbart in disguise with his daughter, Odile. Siegfried thinks she is Odette. As they dance together, Siegfried declares he will love her forever. A vision of Odette appears at the window, Von Rothbart and Odile laugh triumphantly, and Siegfried realizes he has been tricked into breaking his promise to Odette.

Odette and the other swan-maidens are dancing sadly by the lake. Siegfried arrives and begs Odette to forgive him, which she does. But Von Rothbart now has the swan-maidens in his power forever. In desperation, Siegfried and Odette throw themselves in the lake, and at last the spell is broken by the power of their love for one another.

The Firebird
1910, Paris
choreography:
Michel Fokine
music: Igor Stravinsky

The evil magician Kotschei has imprisoned a Princess and her 11 companions in an enchanted garden. Prince Ivan climbs over the wall and, seeing a beautiful Firebird, captures her. In exchange for her release, she gives him one of her feathers, promising to return if he is ever in danger. Ivan hides to watch the princess as she dances with her friends, with golden apples they shake from the trees. He falls in love with her but is captured by Kotschei and his hideous creatures. Ivan summons the Firebird, who shows him how to destroy the magician by smashing a large egg containing his soul. Kotschei's creatures are now freed from the spell that has imprisoned them. Ivan and the princess are crowned king and queen amid great celebration by all who were once Kotschei's prisoners.

Petrushka
1911, Paris
choreography: Fokine
music: Stravinsky

It is Butterweek Fair in St. Petersburg, Russia. A Showman is there, with three lifesize puppets—a Ballerina, a Moor, and a clown called Petrushka. They perform for the crowds.

When the show is over and the puppets are back in their booths, the Ballerina makes fun of Petrushka and the Showman ill-treats him. In his frustration, Petrushka beats his fists on the wall of his booth.

The Ballerina visits the Moor, followed by the jealous Petrushka. The Moor chases Petrushka out of the booth and strikes him with a scimitar. To the crowd's horror, Petrushka appears to bleed, but the Showman lifts up the limp body and shows them it is only a puppet, leaking sawdust.

As night falls and the Fair closes, the ghost of Petrushka rises above the sideshow, taunting the Showman.

Cinderella

1948, London
choreography:
Frederick Ashton
music: Sergei Prokofiev

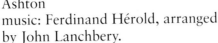

Cinderella's two wicked stepsisters (traditionally men dressed up as women) set out for the palace ball, leaving Cinderella behind. In rags, with her broom as partner, she dreams of dancing. Suddenly her Fairy Godmother arrives with the fairies of the four seasons. She casts magic spells so that Cinderella can go to the ball in a beautiful dress—but warns Cinderella that she must come home at midnight.

At the ball, Cinderella descends the staircase en pointe and dances with the Prince. On the stroke of midnight she rushes out, losing one of her slippers. The Prince vows to marry the girl whose foot it fits.

Back home, the stepsisters try to squash their huge feet into the tiny slipper. Cinderella shyly tries the slipper—it fits, and the Prince marries her, to the dismay of her two stepsisters.

La Fille Mal Gardée

1960, London
choreography:
Ashton
music: Ferdinand Hérold, arranged by John Lanchbery.

This is based on a very old French ballet, first performed in Bordeaux in 1789. Lise and her mother, Widow Simone (played by a man), live on a farm in France. Lise is in love with Colas. Widow Simone introduces Alain, son of wealthy Farmer Thomas, but Lise is not impressed.

At the harvest, Lise and Colas dance with their friends, Widow Simone does a comical clog dance, and then everyone dances around a maypole.

Back at home, harvesters bring in sheaves of wheat. Colas jumps out from the wheat, and Lise hides him in her room. Widow Simone brings Alain to marry Lise, and Colas is discovered. Widow Simone finally relents, and agrees to Lise marrying Colas.

Romeo and Juliet

1965, London
choreography:
MacMillan
music: Prokofiev

This ballet is based on Shakespeare's play. Two families in Verona, Italy, have been ordered to end their feud. The Montagues have a son, Romeo. The Capulets have a daughter, Juliet, and a nephew, Tybalt. At a masked ball, Romeo falls in love with Juliet. They meet beneath Juliet's balcony and declare their love for each other.

In a small chapel, with Juliet's nursemaid as witness, the lovers are married. But fighting breaks out. Tybalt kills a friend of Romeo's, and Romeo kills Tybalt and flees the city.

Juliet's parents have arranged for her to marry Paris. In despair, she takes a drug that will make her look dead, when really only asleep.

The Capulets discover Juliet's body and lay her in the family vault. Romeo enters the vault. Thinking Juliet is dead, he takes poison. Juliet wakes to find her beloved Romeo dead at her side, and stabs herself.

Enjoying ballet

You don't have to go to ballet classes to enjoy ballet. There are lots of other ways to become a knowledgeable ballet fan.

Watching ballet

You can start by watching ballet on television and video. You will enjoy it much more if you read the story first and listen to some of the music.

▼ Meeting dancers and collecting autographs after the show

Ask yourself questions about what you see. Was it well danced? If so, what made it special? What if it wasn't so good? What might have made it better?

Keeping a scrapbook

You can fill a scrapbook with clippings about ballet and pictures of your favorite dancers cut from newspapers, magazines, and publicity material.

Writing a review

Watch for reviews by critics who write about the performances. Do you agree with them?

Try to write your own brief review of something you have seen. How would you describe it to somebody else?

Going to the theater

If you want to watch ballet live, you can start with performances by local ballet schools. If you dance yourself, you can always

learn something by watching others. When a professional ballet company visits your town, try to see them perform. If you go in a group with friends from school or your ballet class, the tickets are usually less expensive. Companies sometimes have talks before the performance, to help explain what you are about to see.

Ballet companies usually have an education officer who will be happy to tell you what they offer—anything from booklets and posters for sale to a place in a workshop where you can learn some of the choreography. You can telephone or write to them at the theater where the company is based.

Workshops

Workshops teach you basic ballet movements, and sometimes help you use these to create your own dances.

Your teacher at school may be able to arrange for dancers from a company to visit, talk about their lives, dance, and teach a workshop.

If you are already dancing, there are summer schools where you can make friends with other dancers, attend classes with different teachers, take part in a performance, or try your hand at choreography.

▼ A school visit by a ballet company may include a workshop on makeup and costume. Kostchei, the evil magician in *The Firebird*, wears great fantasy makeup.

Design your own ballet

Don't forget that ballet is four things in one—dance, music, art, and drama. If you are interested in costume and design, you might like to choose a story and make drawings of ballet scenery and costumes.

▲ A school workshop on pas de deux

If you play an instrument, get together with others and compose some ballet music. You can use a computer to do both of these. Make a cassette or video recording of your work.

If you want to know more about ballet history and famous dancers, use your library—they may lend tapes and videos too.

There are also museums that display costumes, such as Anna Pavlova's Swan tutu, and designs and scores from Diaghilev's company.

Ballet in art

Painters, sculptors, and photographers have always been fascinated by ballet.

Watch for exhibitions of work by painters such as Degas, Dame Laura Knight, and Robert Heindel or photographs by Cecil Beaton or Richard Avedon. You might like to sketch, paint, or photograph ballet yourself, or use clay to capture those elusive positions.

Whatever you choose to do, it will help you to enjoy and understand ballet more.

Finding out

If you are doing a project about ballet or theater, it is a mistake to write to the company with a general request such as "Please send me everything you have."

It is much better to prepare for a project on something more specific and focus on one or two dancers or on a few ballets.

People are much more willing to help if you have already done some preparation and have a clear idea of what you need to complete your project.

Every major theater has its own archive, which is like a museum or library and is looked after by an archivist who makes a catalog of all the material. The archive might include old books, posters, programs, reviews, costumes, photographs, and choreographer's notes.

If you are interested in a particular dancer, choreographer, or ballet, you can write to the archivist for specific information. Sometimes it is even possible to arrange a visit to the archive and see its treasures for yourself.

▼ "Pavlova Taking A Bow," by Dame Laura Knight (1877–1970). Knight loved to paint scenes from the ballet and the circus.

Great dancers of the 20th century

Mikhail Baryshnikov

See page 11.

Darcey Bussell

Born in London in 1969, Bussell trained at The Royal Ballet School and became a principal in 1989. Her dancing combines great virtuosity with a fresh, youthful quality—as in her Aurora for The Royal Ballet's new production of *The Sleeping Beauty*, which was premiered in Washington, D.C., in 1994.

Erik Bruhn

This dancer was known for his superb technique and elegant manner in classical roles, and was one of the very best male dancers. Born in 1928, Bruhn trained at the Royal Danish Ballet School, joining the company in 1937. He danced in the United States, Britain, and Denmark, and directed in Sweden and Canada. He also encouraged dancers to be more informed and responsible about their well-being and careers. He died in 1986.

Suzanne Farrell

Born in 1945, Farrell trained at the American School of Ballet and joined the New York City Ballet at the age of 16. As an N.Y.C.B. star, she was known for her immaculate technique. She danced in many ballets choreographed by George Balanchine, including *Jewels*, *Variations*, and *Union Jack*.

Margot Fonteyn

Born in Britain in 1919, Fonteyn studied at Dame Ninette de Valois' Sadler's Wells school, becoming a soloist with the company at 16. She is remembered for her flawless classical technique and her beauty and elegance as a ballerina. Famous partners include Michael Somes and Rudolf Nureyev, and famous performances include *Swan Lake*, *The Sleeping Beauty*, *Romeo and Juliet*, and *Marguerite and Armand*. Fonteyn died in 1991.

Romeo and Juliet

Sylvie Guillem

Born in 1965, Guillem trained at the Paris Opéra Ballet School, from which she graduated into the company. She is a principal guest artist with The Royal Ballet but also appears with other companies. As a child, Guillem trained as a gymnast. She is known for her extensions and suppleness.

Marcia Haydée

Born in Brazil in 1951, this ballerina created many leading roles for the Stuttgart Ballet under the direction of choreographer John Cranko. She was known for her lyrical dancing and powerful acting. She retired in 1996.

Karen Kain

Born in 1951, she trained at the National Ballet School in Canada, joining the company in 1969. She became a principal dancer in 1971 and has appeared as guest artist with many other leading companies. Kain was one of Nureyev's celebrated partners.

Arthur Mitchell

This former star of the New York City Ballet is the first black classical ballet dancer to gain an international reputation. Born in 1934, Mitchell studied at the High School of Performing Arts and the School of American Ballet before joining Balanchine's company in 1955. For him, Balanchine created the role of Puck in *A Midsummer Night's Dream*. Since 1969 he has been the director of the company he helped to found, the Dance Theatre of Harlem.

Irek Mukhamedov

Mukhamedov trained at the Bolshoi Ballet school, and as a leading dancer with the company was famous for dramatic roles in ballets such as *Spartacus*. In 1990 he joined The Royal Ballet. He is known for his great technical skill and superb acting and has danced in new ballets by a variety of choreographers.

Vaslav Nijinsky

Born in Russia in 1889, Nijinsky trained at the Imperial Russian Ballet School. He joined Diaghilev's Ballets Russes, in which he had a short but legendary career dancing in ballets such as *Le*

The Rite of Spring

Spectre de la Rose, *Petrushka*, and *The Firebird*. He also danced and choreographed two sensational ballets, *The Rite of Spring* and *L'Après-midi d'un Faune*. Nijinsky suffered from mental illness and died in 1950. His diaries and a biography written by his wife give a fascinating insight into his life.

Rudolf Nureyev

Born in 1938 on a train in Russia, Nureyev trained at the Leningrad Ballet School from the age of 17 and at 20 made his debut with the Kirov Ballet. In 1961, Nureyev was invited to join The Royal Ballet. He danced many leading roles, establishing a famous partnership with Margot Fonteyn, and was a virtuoso performer with a magnetic personality. He also choreographed new productions of well-known ballets such as *The Nutcracker, Don Quixote*, and *Romeo and Juliet*. Nureyev became Director of the Paris Opéra Ballet in 1983 and died in 1993.

The Nutcracker

Anna Pavlova
See pages 10–11.

Galina Ulanova

Born in Russia in 1910, this great ballerina danced with both the Kirov and the Bolshoi ballet companies, and was known for her graceful and poignant performances in ballets such as *Giselle* and *Romeo and Juliet*. She went on teach at the Bolshoi Ballet School, coaching students for ballerina roles.

Great teachers

Many teachers have shaped the way ballet has developed. Carlo Blasis was the first man to set out ballet technique as we know it today, in a book called *The Code of Terpsichore*, which was published in 1830. August Bournonville led the Danish ballet from 1830 and created its distinctive ballet technique, including *ballon*—very light, springy jumping. Many schools, especially in Eastern Europe, study the method named after Agrippina Vaganova, a Russian teacher who died in 1951. Other dancers study the Cecchetti method, named after Enrico Cecchetti who taught many famous dancers of the Maryinsky and Diaghilev companies—including Anna Pavlova.

Great composers

Jean Baptiste Lully 1632–1687

One of the first composers for ballet at the court of Louis XIV was a dancer himself and became Director of the Académie Royale de Musique. His ballets include *Le Ballet Royal de la Nuit*, with Louis XIV as the sun god, Apollo.

Léo Delibes 1836–1891

A French composer much admired by Tchaikovsky, Delibes composed *La Source, Sylvia*, and *Coppélia*. In *Coppélia*, he developed the idea, begun by Adam in *Giselle*, of a musical theme for each character.

Frédéric Chopin 1810–1849

Born in Poland, Chopin wrote no ballet music as such, but his music has been used for many ballets. The best known is probably *Les Sylphides* (called *Chopiniana* at first), which was choreographed by Fokine. Jerome Robbins used Chopin's music for *The Concert* and *Dances at a Gathering*, as did Ashton for *A Month in the Country*.

Sergei Prokofiev 1891–1953

This classical composer's ballet music includes *Prodigal Son, The Stone Flower, Cinderella*, and *Romeo and Juliet*. He also wrote operas and film scores.

Igor Stravinsky 1882–1971

This Russian composer worked closely with Diaghilev, Nijinsky, and Balanchine, and wrote music for ballets such as *The Firebird, Petrushka, Les Noces, The Rite of Spring, Apollo*, and *Agon*. Music not specially written for ballet has been used by choreographers such as MacMillan and Robbins.

Pyotr Ilyich Tchaikovsky
1840–1893 See page 26.

Great choreographers of the 20th century

Frederick Ashton

Born in Ecuador, South America, in 1904, Ashton studied with Léonide Massine and Marie Rambert. An outstanding choreographer, he was also Director of The Royal Ballet from 1963 to 1970. Audiences love his ballets for their lyricism, musicality, and imaginative use of classical technique. The Cecchetti method forms the basis of much of his work. Narrative and theme ballets include *Cinderella, Sylvia, La Fille Mal Gardée, Ondine, The Dream, Enigma Variations, The Two Pigeons,* and *A Month in the Country.* Abstract ballets include *Symphonic Variations, Scènes de Ballet,* and *Monotones.* For children, Ashton choreographed the delightful *Tales of Beatrix Potter.* He had the gift of creating characters that came alive on stage. Aston died in 1988.

La Fille Mal Gardée

George Balanchine

Born in St. Petersburg in 1904, Balanchine trained at the Petrograd Imperial Ballet Academy. Diaghilev made him chief choreographer of the Ballets Russes in 1925. He was invited to the United States, where he started the School of American Ballet in 1934, and one year later the best students formed a new company, American Ballet. His next company, The Ballet Society, was the nucleus from which the New York City Ballet grew. Balanchine is one of the greatest choreographers in the history of ballet. His ballets are mostly abstract celebrations of dance, in which his dancers are able to show superb skill, musicality, and the joy of dance. His works include *Concerto Barocco, Theme and Variations, Agon, Apollo, Symphony in C,* and *The Four Temperaments.* Balanchine died in 1983, leaving a world-famous company with a strong, distinctive style.

Maurice Béjart

Born in France in 1924, Béjart founded the Ballet of the Twentieth Century in Brussels in 1960. His work is dramatic and controversial and draws its inspiration from theater and dance from all over the world. He uses large group scenes to create powerful effects and choreographs particularly well for male dancers. His ballets include *The Rite of Spring, Nijinsky— Clown of God,* and *Bolero,* which is set to Ravel's hypnotic music. The company is now based in Lausanne, Switzerland.

John Cranko

Born in South Africa in 1927, Cranko trained at the Sadler's Wells Ballet School and joined the company in 1946. He became Director of the Stuttgart Ballet in 1961 and choreographed many lasting works for Stuttgart and for The Royal Ballet, including the full-length ballets *The Taming of the Shrew* and *Romeo and Juliet,* as well as shorter ballets such as *Pineapple Poll* and *The Lady and the Fool.* Cranko's work is known for its wit, humor, and strong characterization. He died suddenly while on tour in the United States in 1973, leaving the Stuttgart company one of the strongest in Europe.

Apollo

Yuri Grigorovich

Born in Russia in 1927, Grigorovich became chief choreographer and artistic director of the Bolshoi Ballet in 1964. His work is full of strong athletic dancing for the men and elegant virtuoso steps for women. Using scenes from Russian history, he made epic ballets with large crowds and lyrical pas de deux. Such ballets include *The Golden Age,* set in the 1920s; *Ivan the Terrible,* set in 16th-century Russia; and *Spartacus,* about a slave rebellion in Roman times.

Kenneth MacMillan

Born in 1929, MacMillan originally trained as a dancer at the

Elite Syncopations

Sadler's Wells School. In 1946 MacMillan joined the Sadler's Wells Theatre Ballet. He later became a choreographer, and was appointed Resident Choreographer for The Royal Ballet in 1965 and Artistic Director in 1970. He is best known for full-length narrative ballets such as *Romeo and Juliet*, *Anastasia*, *Manon*, and *Mayerling*. But he has also choreographed memorable abstract ballets such as *Elite Syncopations*, *Song of the Earth*, and *Gloria*, which takes its theme from the grief caused by World War I. His ballets use classical technique and dramatic staging to convey complex human emotions, and they have a powerful impact on the audience. MacMillan died in 1992.

Bronislava Nijinska

Born in 1891 in Russia, Bronislava was the sister of Vaslav Nijinsky. She studied with Cecchetti and joined first the Maryinsky company and then the Ballets Russes. She choreographed numerous ballets, including *Renard*, *Les Biches*, and one of the most outstanding, *Les Noces*. Set to music by Stravinsky, and designs by Russian painter Natalia Goncharova, *Les Noces* draws on preparations for a traditional Russian wedding for its theme. Although Bronislava used classical steps, she drew on folk and jazz influences to create ballets in which design, dance, and music blend together to unusual effect.

Jerome Robbins

Born in the United States in 1918, Robbins began his career as a dancer in musicals on Broadway. His first ballet, *Fancy Free*, was set to music by Leonard Bernstein and features three sailors out to enjoy themselves; it was so successful that it became a stage and screen musical called *On the Town*. His classical works are enjoyable celebrations of dance such as *The Concert* and *Dances at a Gathering*, both created for New York City Ballet. But they can also be tense and powerful, like his *Afternoon of a Faun*. This ballet is choreographed to the same Debussy score, *L' Après-midi d'un Faune*, that Nijinsky used in 1912. Set in a ballet studio, it explores the relationship between two dancers. Robbins went on to win an Oscar for his collaboration with Bernstein on the film *West Side Story*, which was first staged as a musical.

Glen Tetley

Born in the United States in 1926, Tetley first

Voluntaries

studied medicine, then danced with Antony Tudor and Martha Graham. He began as a choreographer in the contemporary dance style, with works such as *Pierrot Lunaire*, and then produced more classical ballets, such as *Field Figures* and *Voluntaries*. His works are usually abstract, full of unusual and imaginative movement, shapes and patterns to music by some outstanding modern composers such as Varèse, Berg, Schoenberg, and Henze.

Antony Tudor

Born in 1908, Tudor did not begin dancing until he was 19. He trained at the Rambert School, which was attached to the ballet company founded in the 1930s by Dame Marie Rambert. She had once been a member of Diaghilev's company, and she encouraged many young choreographers such as Ashton, Tudor, and Cranko. Tudor's works had a strong dramatic element and were performed by Ballet Rambert, New York City Ballet, The Royal Ballet, and The Royal Swedish Ballet. They include *Lilac Garden*, *Pillar of Fire*, and *Shadowplay*. *Pillar of Fire* and his last ballet, *Tiller of the Fields*, were both created for American Ballet Theatre. Tudor died in 1987.

Ninette de Valois

De Valois was born in Ireland in 1898 and danced with Diaghilev. She founded the Vic-Wells Ballet in 1931, which led to the Sadler's Wells Theatre Ballet, from which grew The Royal Ballet and Birmingham Royal Ballet. Her works have strong national themes, are full of dramatic and rich choreography, and use British composers and designers. They include *Job*, *Checkmate*, and *The Rake's Progress*, which is based on a series of 18th-century paintings by William Hogarth about the rise and fall of a young man-about-town. During her long career, de Valois has been responsible for noticing and encouraging many other choreographers such as Ashton, Cranko, MacMillan, and David Bintley.

Great companies

American Ballet Theatre

After Anna Pavlova's partner, Mikhail Mordkin, toured his small company in the United States, some of his Russian dancers, led by Lucia Chase and Richard Pleasant, formed Ballet Theatre in 1939. The company (later named American Ballet Theater) became a center-piece of the American ballet tradition, with such guest dancers as Erik Bruhn, Natalia Makarova, and Gelsey Kirkland. It has staged successful works by choreographers such as Mikhail Fokine, George Balanchine, Agnes de Mille, Glen Tetley, Twyla Tharp, Jerome Robbins, and Antony Tudor. In 1980, Mikhail Baryshnikov became A.B.T.'s Director. The company is now led by Kevin Mckenzie.

Australian Ballet

The company as it is known today was founded by Ninette de Valois' assistant, Peggy van Praagh, in 1962. In 1965, Robert Helpmann, an early partner of Margot Fonteyn, became its Director. The company is based in Melbourne and has its own school. It presents strong productions of the classics as well as new work and tours worldwide.

Birmingham Royal Ballet

When it moved into Covent Garden in 1946, The Royal Ballet had a touring section which visited theaters all over Great Britain and abroad. In the 1970s part of this touring company was based once again at Sadler's Wells Theatre, where it was called The Sadler's Wells Royal Ballet, under the direction of Sir Peter Wright. In 1990, the company moved to Birmingham, in England, where it is based at the Hippodrome theater. David Bintley, choreographer of popular ballets such as *The Snow Queen* and *Hobson's Choice*, was appointed Director in 1995.

Bolshoi Theater

The Bolshoi Ballet

This world-famous Russian company probably began with a ballet class which opened at a Moscow orphanage in 1774 to provide dancers for the Petrovsky Theater. The company has been based at the Bolshoi Theater since 1856. Carlo Blasis taught at the school in the 1860s. The company performed the very first *Swan Lake*, and Marius Petipa created *Don Quixote* for it in 1869. The Bolshoi's dramatic and flamboyant style emerged in the 1930s, under the direction of Leonid Lavrovsky. The company now tours worldwide.

Sydney Opera House

Dance Theatre of Harlem

This company, founded by former New York City Ballet principal dancer Arthur Mitchell and Karel Shook, was the first ballet company to develop black classical dancers. It was founded in 1968 and made its debut in 1971 at the Guggenheim Museum in New York City with three Mitchell ballets. The company went on to perform ballets by Balanchine, Tetley, and Geoffrey Holder, as well as new versions of *The Firebird* (set on a tropical island) and *Giselle* (set in Louisiana).

English National Ballet

Dame Alicia Markova and Sir Anton Dolin, both former dancers with Diaghilev, gathered together a group of dancers in 1949. From this grew Festival Ballet, which had its first performance in 1950. In 1968 the company became known as London Festival Ballet. Performing regularly at London's Festival Hall, the company toured widely. Early productions included *Witch Boy*, *Peer Gynt*, and *Etudes*. Now called English National Ballet, the company is currently led by Derek Deane, former Royal Ballet principal.

The Kirov Ballet

This renowned Russian company was founded in St. Petersburg in 1783. By the late 1800s, the company was performing at the Maryinsky Theater, drawing its pupils from the famous ballet academy on Theater Street. Petipa produced *The Sleeping Beauty*, *The Nutcracker*, *Swan Lake*, and *Raymonda* for the company.

At the turn of the century, its most famous dancers were Preobajenska, Pavlova, Karsavina, and Nijinsky. The company survived the Russian Revolution and toured abroad. Under the direction of Sergeyev, the company emphasized the preservation of the classics. It lost many of its leading dancers such as Nureyev, Makarova, and Baryshnikov to the West.

National Ballet of Canada

This company, founded in 1951, is based in Toronto. Its first Director was Celia Franca, followed by Alexander Grant—both British dancers. Grant introduced Frederick Ashton's ballets into the wide repertoire. Danish star Erik Bruhn was Artistic Director from 1983 to 1986. There is a ballet school attached to the company.

New York City Ballet

American writer and arts patron Lincoln Kirstein invited George Balanchine to open a ballet school, with the dream of its becoming America's first ballet company. It began presenting ballets in New York in the 1940s, and in 1964 New York City Ballet moved into the State Theater at Lincoln Center. Its great dancers have included Jacques d'Amboise, Melissa Hayden, Maria Tallchief, and Edward Villella. Although the Balanchine ballets are central to the company's repertoire, preserved by the Balanchine Trust, it performs many new works and is currently under the direction of

Metropolitan Opera House, New York

an outstanding former dancer and choreographer, Peter Martins. The New York City Ballet School is one of the most famous in the world.

Palais Garnier, Paris

Paris Opéra Ballet

The company can be traced back to Louis XIV and the Académie Royale de Danse, which opened a training establishment in 1713. Among the first stars were Camargo and Sallé, followed by Vestris and Noverre. Romantic ballerinas Taglioni and Elssler made their début at the Paris Opéra in the 1830s. The company moved to its present home in the Palais Garnier in 1875. Rudolf Nureyev directed the company from 1983 until his death. There is a school attached to the company, whose pupils were traditionally known as *Les Petits Rats* ("the little rats").

The Royal Ballet

The company grew out of the Sadler's Wells Ballet School, founded at Sadler's Wells Theatre in London by Dame Ninette de Valois in the 1930s. At first it was called the Vic-Wells Ballet. In 1946 the company, then called the Sadler's Wells Theatre Ballet, moved into The Royal Opera House, Covent Garden, with a new production of *The Sleeping Beauty*. It became The Royal Ballet in 1956. The company has a school attached to it, The Royal Ballet School, directed by former ballerina Dame Merle Park. Its current Artistic Director is Anthony Dowell, a superb classical dancer who trained at the school and danced many leading roles with The Royal Ballet.

The Royal Opera House, London

The Royal Danish Ballet

When this famous company was established in Copenhagen in 1784, there had been a court ballet in Denmark since the 16th century. When August Bournonville, a student of Vestris, became ballet master in 1830, he was able to establish the distinctive style which still exists today. Bournonville ballets still cherished by the company include *Napoli*, *La Sylphide*, and *Konservatoriet*, which recreates a ballet class with Vestris.

The Stuttgart Ballet

Choreographer Jean Georges Noverre was the first to lead this court ballet, from 1760 to 1766. More recently, it began to attract worldwide recognition with John Cranko as Director in 1960—this established its reputation for exciting and lively choreography. The company's school is known for its high standards.

Ballet in history

Ballet has changed a great deal through the ages. The changes were part of many other things that happened in history—how people lived, what battles they fought, even what they wore and ate.

1462 First known writing about dance technique, by Domenico di Piacenza. Italian courts hold lavish dance entertainments.

1581 The first known ballet, *Le Ballet Comique de la Reine*, is performed at a royal marriage in France, from 10p.m. to 3a.m.

1588 Arbeau's *Orchesographie* is the first French writing about dance technique.

1608 Cosimo de' Medici holds a horse ballet in Florence, Italy.

1620 *Mayflower* Pilgrims land in Massachusetts.

1642–1646 Civil War in England (Roundheads—Parliamentarians versus Cavaliers—Royalists).

1653 Louis XIV dances as the sun god, Apollo, in *Le Ballet Royal de la Nuit*, France.

Louis XIV

1661 Louis XIV founds the Académie Royale de Danse, France.

1669 The Académie Royale de Musique is founded, France.

1681 First female dancers appear on stage in Jean Baptiste Lully's *Le Triomphe de l'Amour*, France. (One of the ballerinas, Mademoiselle de Lafontaine, is said to have danced for 10 years and then become a nun.)

1717 John Weaver's *Loves of Mars and Venus* is staged in London.

1727 Marie Camargo shortens her skirts, France.

1738 Imperial Ballet School is founded, in St. Petersburg, Russia.

1758 Jean Georges Noverre produces two early *ballets d'action*, *Les Caprices de Galathée* and *La Toilette de Venus*, France.

1762 Catherine the Great becomes Empress of Russia.

1774 Bolshoi Ballet School is founded in Moscow.

1776 The Declaration of Independence is signed.

1781 Noverre becomes ballet master at King's Theatre, London.

1789 French Revolution begins.

1801 Salvatore Vigano presents *The Creatures of Prometheus* in Vienna, with Beethoven's only ballet score.

1804 Napoleon is crowned Emperor of France.

1815 Battle of Waterloo.

1830 August Bournonville becomes ballet master of the Royal Danish Ballet. Carlo Blasis publishes *The Code of Terpsichore*

Marie Camargo

in London.

1832 Marie Taglioni dances *La Sylphide*—the beginning of Romantic ballet. (Russian admirers later cook her shoes in a stew.)

1837 Coronation of Queen Victoria.

1840 Fanny Elssler is the first Romantic ballerina to tour the United States.

1841 First performance of *Giselle*, Paris.

1845 Four stars of Romantic ballet (Fanny Cerrito, Lucile Grahn, Carlotta Grisi, and Marie Taglioni) dance their famous *Pas de Quatre*.

1861–1865 The Civil War.

1862 A rising star in Paris, Emma Livry, refuses to wear a fire-resistant tutu because it is not pure white; her skirts catch fire in rehearsal and she dies from her burns.

1869 Marius Petipa is appointed First Ballet Master to the Tsar's Imperial Ballet, St. Petersburg. First performance of *Don Quixote*, Moscow.

1870 First performance of *Coppélia*, Paris. Franco-Prussian War begins—siege of Paris.

1877 First performance of *Swan Lake*, in Moscow, is not a success—but it will be revived in 1895 in St. Petersburg.

1881 Edgar Degas exhibits a lifelike wax sculpture called "The Little Dancer."

1890 First performance of *The Sleeping Beauty*, St. Petersburg.

1892 First performance

Carabosse, in *The Sleeping Beauty*

of *The Nutcracker*, St. Petersburg.

1895 First performance of 32 fouettés in *Swan Lake*, by Pierina Legnani in St. Petersburg.

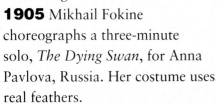

Pavlova

1905 Mikhail Fokine choreographs a three-minute solo, *The Dying Swan*, for Anna Pavlova, Russia. Her costume uses real feathers.

1909 First season of Serge Diaghilev's Ballets Russes, Paris—in the next two seasons, *The Firebird* and *Petrushka* will be smash hits.

1910 Léon Bakst designs *Schéhérazade* for Diaghilev, Paris.

1911 Alexandre Benois designs *Petrushka* for Diaghilev, Paris.

Petrushka

1913 First performance of Vaslav Nijinsky's *Rite of Spring* in Paris, to music by Igor Stravinsky—a riot breaks out in the theater.

1914–1918 World War I.

1916 Ballet Russes performs in New York.

1917 Jean Cocteau designs Cubist ballet, *Parade*, for Diaghilev —music by Erik Satie (including ships' sirens and a typewriter) and choreography by Léonide Massine. Russian Revolution.

1919 Nijinsky's last performance.

1920 19th Amendment to Constitution gives women the vote.

1928 First performance of George Balanchine's *Apollo*, Paris.

1929 Death of Diaghilev in Venice, Italy.

1931 Ninette de Valois becomes Director of Vic-Wells Ballet, London.

1934 Balanchine and Kirstein open School of American Ballet. Margot Fonteyn's first role is a snowflake in *The Nutcracker*—she will retire at the age of 60.

1939–1945 World War II.

1939 Ballet Theatre (later American Ballet Theatre) is founded. First performance by Ballet Rambert, founded by Marie Rambert, U.K.

1940 First performance of Leonid Lavrovsky's *Romeo and Juliet*, Leningrad (St. Petersburg).

1944 First performance of Jerome Robbins's *Fancy Free*, by Ballet Theatre, New York.

1945 Balanchine choreographs a circus polka for elephants, to music by Stravinsky. Founding of the United Nations, New York.

1946 Sadler's Wells Ballet moves to Covent Garden, London.

1948 First performance of Frederick Ashton's *Cinderella*, London.

1950 Alicia Markova and Anton Dolin form Festival Ballet, London.

1951 National Ballet of Canada is founded, Toronto.

1953 Coronation of Queen Elizabeth II.

1956 Sadler's Wells Ballet becomes The Royal Ballet.

1957 Treaty of Rome establishes the European Community.

La Fille Mal Gardée

1960 John Cranko becomes Director of the Stuttgart Ballet. First performance of Ashton's *La Fille Mal Gardée*, London. The Robert Joffrey Ballet is founded, New York.

1962 Nureyev joins The Royal Ballet. Australian Ballet is founded.

1964 Civil Rights Bill passed in U.S. Martin Luther King receives the Nobel Peace Prize.

1965 Flemming Flindt becomes Director of the Royal Danish Ballet. First performance of Kenneth MacMillan's *Romeo and Juliet*, London.

1968 First performance of Yuri Grigorovich's *Spartacus*, Moscow.

1969 First performance of Cranko's *Taming of the Shrew*, Stuttgart. Astronauts Neil Armstrong and Buzz Aldrin become the first men to walk on the Moon.

1971 Dance Theatre of Harlem makes debut in New York.

1974 Mikhail Baryshnikov defects to the West and joins American Ballet Theatre. First performance of MacMillan's *Elite Syncopations*, London.

1983 Nureyev becomes Director of the Paris Opéra Ballet. Peter Martins and Jerome Robbins become co-directors of New York City Ballet. Peter Schaufuss becomes Director of London's Festival Ballet.

1986 Anthony Dowell becomes Director of The Royal Ballet.

1989 Berlin Wall comes down.

1990 Bolshoi star Irek Mukhamedov joins The Royal Ballet. Sadler's Wells Royal Ballet becomes Birmingham Royal Ballet.

1991 Death of Fonteyn. Break-up of Soviet Union.

1993 Death of Nureyev.

1995 A ballet fan buys a pair of Nureyev's ballet shoes at an auction for $18,700. Modern dance choreographer Twyla Tharp creates a ballet for The Royal Ballet.

Glossary

abstract ballet Ballet with no story or dramatic theme—dance for its own sake.

adage *ad-ahge* Slow and sustained steps and movements which flow from one to the other.

alignment Relationship of one part of the body to another.

allegro *al-leg-row* Fast and lively steps which may include jumps and traveling steps. There is grand (large) and petit (small) allegro.

arabesque *arab-esk* The dancer balances on one leg with the other stretched and raised behind.

attitude *at-ee-tood* Somewhat like an arabesque except that the lifted leg is bent at the knee in a curve behind the body.

arabesque

auditorium Part of the theater where the audience sits.

backdrop Painted cloth which hangs down at the back of the stage as part of the scenery.

ballet d'action Form of 18th-century ballet which used mime and acting, instead of masks and other old conventions, to tell the story.

ballet de cour Court ballet of the 17th century with sumptuous costumes, music, dance, mime, and processions.

ballet master Runs rehearsals, and sometimes organizes them.

ballet mistress Runs rehearsals. Usually responsible for rehearsing female corps de ballet.

ballon A style of jumping in a particular "bouncy" way, so that the dancer seems to hover in the air.

barre A wooden rail, fixed to the walls of a dance studio. The dancers use it to help them balance while they practice basic exercises.

battements frappés *bat-mon frap-ay* A barre exercise in which the foot is first flexed and then struck against the floor, like a match against a box.

battements tendues *bat-mon ton-doo* A barre exercise in which the foot is stretched along the floor until it points.

batterie *battery* Steps in which the legs are beaten together, such as an entrechat. There is petite (small) batterie and grande (large) batterie.

Benesh notation A way of recording dance steps. Invented by Joan and Rudolf Benesh in 1955.

changement *shonge-mon* A small jump which begins in fifth position with one foot in front and ends in fifth position with the other foot in front. Used as a basis for learning entrechats.

character dancing When traditional folk dances are choreographed for ballets, they are called character dances—an example is the Polish mazurka staged in *Coppélia*.

character role A part in a ballet which involves acting and mime rather than dance, such as the Queen in *Swan Lake* and Carabosse in *The Sleeping Beauty*.

choreographer The person who has the idea for the ballet and then arranges the steps and patterns so that they make a whole work of art.

classical ballet The style of dance based on rules laid down over centuries by French, Russian, Danish, and Italian teachers and schools.

Classical ballets Usually Russian story ballets of the late 19th century which follow a particular pattern—such as *Swan Lake* and *The Sleeping Beauty*.

contemporary dance A 20th-century dance style which has different rules from ballet. For example, there is no point work, feet can flex instead of point, and ribs and hips have different, less rigid alignments.

corps de ballet *core de ballay* Dancers who perform together as a group and do not dance solos or leading roles.

coryphée *corry-fay* A junior soloist, somewhere between the corps de ballet and soloist rank.

divertissement *dee-ver-tiss-mon* A display of dancing that is not central to the story of a ballet—such as the solos Dawn and Prayer in Act II of *Coppélia*, and Puss-in-Boots and the other wedding dances in Act III of *The Sleeping Beauty*.

divertissement

demi-caractère Dancing, or a dancer, with a comic or folk dance flavor, often technically gifted. Examples are Puck in *The Dream* and Alain in *La Fille Mal Gardée*.

en avant *on av-on* Forward, as in fifth en avant, where the arms are held in front or forward.

demi-caractère

enchaînement *on-shane-mon* A series of steps linked together, like words making a sentence.

en croix *on krwa* In the shape of a cross, as in a barre exercise when the movement is made forward, to the side, to the back, and to the side again.

en derrière *on derry-air* Backward, the opposite of en avant.

en diagonale *on dee-ag-on-ahl* Dancing that goes diagonally from corner to corner of a studio or stage.

entrechat six *on-tre-sha sees* A jump from fifth position in which straight legs cross over each other three times.

finale The end of a ballet, or in a gala program the climax to a series of divertissements.

flat A piece of painted scenery that stands upright at the side of the stage.

folk dance Dance of people all around the world as a part of everyday life. It is passed down through the generations and does not use a choreographer or complicated staging.

folk dance

fouetté *fwet-ay* A turn in which the working leg seems to whip in a circular movement away from the supporting leg—like a spoon in a bowl of cake batter. Odile performs a series of 32 fouettés in Act III of *Swan Lake*.

grand allegro *grond allegro* Large jumping and traveling steps.

grands battements *gron bat-mon* A barre exercise in which the leg sweeps up to waist height or higher and is lowered in a more controlled way. Usually practiced en croix.

grand jeté *gron shet-ay* A large traveling jump, with legs outstretched.

grand jeté

jazz dance Began in America around 1917. Based on African dance movements and developed alongside jazz music. Many choreographers have used jazz dance in ballets, especially Jerome Robbins.

Labanotation A system of recording dance steps and ordinary movement, developed by Rudolf von Laban.

leotard Close-fitting costume, like a swimsuit, with or without sleeves, worn for ballet classes.

line The graceful curves and shapes made by a dancer's body in the space around them.

lyricism A way of dancing which is particularly graceful and flowing.

leotard

motif (or leitmotif) A phrase of movement or music, or an idea. It is repeated throughout a ballet, either to help tell the story or make a pattern the audience can recognize. Examples are *Giselle*, in which each character has their own music, and *La Fille Mal Gardée*, in which ribbons are used in different ways throughout the ballet.

neo-classical Sometimes used to describe ballets developed by George Balanchine, based on Marius Petipa's classical ballets of the late 19th century.

notator Person who records the steps and movements of a ballet using Laban or Benesh notation.

pas de deux *pah deh duh* A dance for two people in ballet, usually male and female. Can be called a duet if they are of the same sex.

petit allegro *petty al-leg-ro* Small jumping and traveling steps performed in enchaînements.

physical therapist A person who treats injured people, including dancers.

pirouette en dedans *piroo-ette on deh-don.* A turn in which the dancer turns inward, toward the supporting leg.

pirouette en dehors *piroo-ette on day-or* A turn in which a dancer turns outward, away from the supporting leg.

plié *plee-ay* A basic ballet movement in which the knees bend.

point work Dancing on the tips of the toes, en pointe, using specially hardened shoes. Performed only by women, except to give a special effect in a demi-caractère role, such as Bottom, when he is a donkey in Frederick Ashton's *The Dream*.

en pointe

port de bras *por deh brah* The movement of the arms in ballet.

premier danseur Principal male dancer in a ballet company.

présage lift A lift in pas de deux in which the male dancer holds the female high above him with his arms straight.

prima ballerina Principal female dancer in a ballet company.

promenade *prom-en-ahd* Sometimes part of pas de deux. The male dancer walks around the female, supporting her while she is en pointe in an arabesque or attitude.

repertoire The collection of ballets that are performed by a company. Students will be expected to learn some of the repertoire as part of their training. Sometimes known as repertory.

répétiteur Teaches the repertoire and takes rehearsals with the company. Usually a former dancer.

révérence Formal bow made by dancers at the end of a class or a performance.

Romantic ballets Ballets that are part of the Romantic movement in the early 19th century. They are usually mysterious fairy stories.

révérence

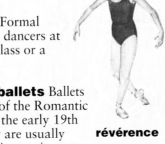

rosin Yellow crystallized chunks of distilled turpentine (a natural resin from trees) which are crushed to a white sticky powder. Used on ballet shoes to stop dancers from slipping on the stage. Kept on a flat tray in the studio and in the wings during a performance.

score

score The complete set of music or dance notation for a ballet.

social dance Dance for pleasure such as ballroom and disco. Court dance was social dance at first, before it was made more formal and became performance dance for audiences.

solo A dance for one person.

spotting Used by dancers to avoid becoming giddy while turning. Your eyes fix on one spot and try to return to the spot as quickly as possible.

technique Means two things. First, the features that are important to classical ballet, such as the steps, turn-out, pointe work. Second, the skill with which a dancer performs these.

tempo The speed at which music is played.

temps de poisson *tom deh pwass-on* A leap in which the body curves in the air, like a fish jumping out of water.

theme ballets Ballets that have no story as such but are clearly about something. Examples are MacMillan's *Gloria*, about the horrors of World War I, and Ashton's *Les Patineurs*, about skating.

turn-out The way the dancer's leg turns out from the hip socket. Central to ballet technique.

tutu The ballerina's skirt made of many layers of gathered net, which can be very short (Classical) or calf-length (Romantic).

understudy The person learning a role who can stand in for another dancer in case of illness or injury.

variation A dancer's solo, sometimes part of a pas de deux, sometimes part of divertissements.

virtuoso A performer or performance of brilliant technical skill.

Index

Acknowledgments

The publishers would like to thank the following
illustrators for their contribution to this book:

Victor Ambrus (Virgil Pomfret Agency) 22–23, 32–33;
Julian Baker 56–57; Peter Dennis (Linda Rogers Associates)
36–37; Francesca D'Ottavi 34–35; Susan Field 46–49;
Terry Gabbey (Associated Freelance Artists Ltd.) 28c/bl, 29tl/bl,
30tr/c/br, 31bl/tr; Pamela Goodchild (B. L. Kearley Ltd.) 9tl,
19br, 21br, 41c, 42bl, 43tr/bl, 50–51; Adam and Christa Hook
(Linden Artists) 24–25; Christian Hook 31bl, 40–41; Biz Hull
(Artist Partners) 12–13, 13br, 14bl, 14–15, 15tr/cr, 16tr, 16–17c,
17t, 18br, 20tr; John James (Temple Rogers Artists Agency)
38–39; Nicki Palin 6–7; Helen Parsley (John Martin Artists) 8,
9br, 44–45; Clive Spong (Linden Artists) 4–5; Jean Paul Tibbles
(Central Illustration Agency) 10–11, 20b, 42r; Shirley Tourret
(B. L. Kearley Ltd.) 9cr, 14t, 15b, 17r, 18t/bl, 19t/cr, 21t/bl, 27t,
29br, 31br, 36l, 37tl/r, 43br.
Border ribbon and Sleeping Beauty miniatures by Ian Beck.

The publishers would also like to thank the following
for supplying photographs for this book:

Ancient Art and Architecture 7; Bridgeman Art Library 8, 25,
51; Bill Cooper 21; Anthony Crickmay 5, 19; e t archive 28, 30;
Mary Evans Picture Library 26t; Novosti Photo Library 31;
Society for Co-operation in Russian and Soviet Studies 26b;
Tate Gallery 13; Reg Wilson 11;

and The Benesh Institute, Anthony Crickmay, English National
Ballet, Robbie Jack, London City Ballet, The Metropolitan
Opera, The Royal Ballet, and The Scottish Ballet for
their kind assistance.

The publishers gratefully acknowledge permission to reproduce
the following copyright material:

page 10, from The Magic of Dance by Margot Fonteyn © 1979
Fountain Productions Ltd., by permission of the author's estate;
page 34, from Nureyev—An Autobiography With Pictures ©
1962 Opera Mundi, by permission of Hodder Headline plc.